The Fall of Reza Shah

This book is dedicated to the memory of my father, K. S. Bakhash,
To my nephew, Abood, who followed the path the son did not, and
To my granddaughters, Ariana and Karenna, who will choose a path of
their own.

The Fall of Reza Shah

*The Abdication, Exile, and Death
of Modern Iran's Founder*

Shaul Bakhash

I.B. TAURIS
LONDON • NEW YORK • OXFORD • NEW DELHI • SYDNEY

I.B. TAURIS
Bloomsbury Publishing Plc
50 Bedford Square, London, WC1B 3DP, UK
1385 Broadway, New York, NY 10018, USA
29 Earlsfort Terrace, Dublin 2, Ireland

BLOOMSBURY, I.B. TAURIS and the I.B. Tauris logo are
trademarks of Bloomsbury Publishing Plc

First published in Great Britain 2021
This paperback edition published 2022

Cover design: ianrossdesigner.com
Cover image © Popperfoto/Getty Images

A catalogue record for this book is available from the British Library.

A catalog record for this book is available from the Library of Congress.

ISBN: PB: 978-0-7556-3809-3
ePDF: 978-0-7556-3503-0
eBook: 978-0-7556-3504-7

Typeset by Newgen KnowledgeWorks Pvt. Ltd., Chennai, India
Printed and bound in Great Britain

Contents

Acknowledgments

I need to thank the friends who read all or several chapters of this book in draft and helped me with their advice and comments: Fereydoun Ala, Jack Censer, Reza Ghotbi, and Hassanali Mehran. In particular, I need to thank my wife, Haleh Esfandiari, who not only read the manuscript, and read it more than once, but who also accompanied me at every step as this book was being researched and written.

The author wishes to acknowledge and thank the following journals, in which earlier versions of a number of the chapters of this book initially appeared: *Middle Eastern Studies*, the *British Journal of Middle Eastern Studies*, *Iranian Studies*, and *Iran Nameh*.

1

Soldier and King, Reformer and Autocrat

At the turn of the Iranian New Year in March 1941, Reza Shah, the autocratic ruler of Iran for sixteen years and the virtual master of Iran for even longer—twenty years—could look back with some satisfaction at what he had already accomplished: nothing less than the transformation of his country. Yet, ever restless, he was pushing for more—more modern factories, more railroad lines, more paved roads, more electrification, more equipment for his beloved army. The one cloud on the horizon was the war raging in Europe; but by declaring Iran's neutrality, he believed he had protected Iran from entanglement in the conflict and its ravages. In this, he gravely misjudged what lay ahead for his country and for himself.

Reza Shah's rise to the pinnacle of power in Iran had been stunning. Born in 1876 or 1877 to a family of modest means, he grew up in Alasht, a small village nestled on the slopes of the Alborz Mountains north of Tehran. His father, who had served as an officer in the Qajar army, died when Reza was still an infant. He was raised by his mother, a woman whose family had immigrated to Iran from the Caucasus. She was helped by an uncle then serving in the Cossack Brigade. The brigade was a Russian-trained, Russian-officered outfit of about three thousand men, established in 1878 and the only effective military force in the country. Reza joined the Cossacks in his early teens and rose rapidly through the ranks. By age 40, Reza Khan, as he was then known, was commander of the Hamadan *otryad* (detachment) of the Cossacks.

He took part in a number of campaigns against unruly tribes and, later, local breakaway movements. It was in this period that he grew acutely aware of the unhappy state of his country.

The Iran Reza Khan would take over in 1921 was in a state of disorder and decline. The problems were legion. The young Ahmad Shah Qajar was inexperienced, timorous, greedy for money, and always impatient to leave Iran, preferring the pleasures of Paris to the drabness of Tehran. The central government was weak, and the large tribal areas were beyond its control. The leading politicians running the government and ministries were divided and ineffective; six cabinets changed hands in a brief nineteen-month period. Revenues were inadequate to meet even basic expenses, and the government relied on British subsidies both to keep the government going and to pay and maintain the Cossack Brigade. Plans to establish a national army had gone nowhere, despite the assignment of British advisers and the injection of British money.

Russian officers commanding the Cossack Brigade often acted in the interests of their own government, not in the interest of Iran. Aside from the Cossack Brigade and a small Central Brigade stationed in the capital, Iran had no military forces to speak of. The Cossack Brigade, as noted, was Russian-officered; the gendarmerie, a force charged with maintaining internal order in the countryside, was Swedish-officered. Its pay was often in arrears; the men were ill-clothed and ill-equipped and, according to a British diplomat, by 1920 the gendarmerie had practically "ceased to exist." Reviewing the men of the Cossack Brigade in October 1920, the new British commander of British forces in Iran, General Edmund Ironside, found even the men of this favored unit to be "in a pitiable condition." Both officers and men lacked winter clothing; many lacked boots and had wrapped their feet in sacking.[1] The roads between major cities were unsafe for travelers or the transport of goods.

Iran's great power neighbors, Britain and Russia, interfered in internal affairs, including, in the case of Britain, in the making and unmaking of cabinets and the selection of the prime minister. During the First World War, the government proved unable to prevent British, Russian (then Bolshevik), and, briefly, Ottoman troops from using Iranian territory to pursue their own strategic interests. The British established the South Persia Rifles (SPR) to maintain order and protect British interests in the south; the East Persia Cordon to guard the approaches to India against incursions from Central Asia; and the North Persia Force (Norperforce), with headquarters in Qazvin, just north of the capital, to guard against possible Bolshevik intrusions from the Caucasus and to keep secure the border area and roads leading from Iraq to Iran. Only in the case of the SPR had the British bothered to secure the Iranian government's formal (and very grudging) agreement. The turmoil of the Russian revolution spilled over into Iran. When the White Russian officer Anton Denikin fled with his ships to take refuge in the Iranian port of Enzeli in the spring of 1921, Bolshevik forces attacked and occupied the port. Fear of a full-scale Bolshevik invasion was widespread; and Europeans were already fleeing the capital. In brief, Iran was not master of its own fate.

Domestic forces also threatened the central government. A rebel with radical leanings, Mirza Kuchik Khan, had raised the banner of rebellion in the city of Rasht. He wrote an admiring letter to Lenin, received Bolshevik assistance, declared a "soviet republic" in the whole of the province of Gilan, and threatened to spread his movement across the entire Caspian littoral. In the northeastern province of Azarbaijan, Mohammad Khiabani, a socialist, a nationalist, and a former member of the Majlis, or Parliament, seized control of the provincial capital, Tabriz, renamed the province Azadistan (the land of freedom), and, before he was defeated and killed, progressed from advocating provincial autonomy to flirting with separation from Iran. In Khorasan, in northwestern Iran, a gendarmerie officer, Mohammad Taqi Pesyan, also rebelled against the central government.

Corruption was widespread. Provincial governors squeezed the peasants to recoup the money they had paid the shah and officials to secure their appointments. Funds the British had advanced to maintain the Cossack Brigade went into the pockets of the shah and the brigade's Russian officers. The officers skimmed the pay of the soldiers to line their own pockets and to share with politicians in Tehran, and the commanding officer kept on the books one thousand men who received pay but did not exist.[2] A particularly striking example of the depth of corruption was the negotiation leading to the Anglo-Persian Agreement of 1919.

The agreement, the brainchild of the British foreign secretary, Lord Curzon, and his minister in Tehran, Percy Cox, envisaged extensive involvement of England in the affairs of Iran. The British were to appoint advisors with wide powers to reorganize the finances and revamp virtually all major government departments. Military advisers would help train and equip a proper military force, and a £2,000,000 British loan would help finance economic development and railway and other transportation projects. Britain's chosen instrument on the Iranian side to form a government friendly to Britain and to negotiate, conclude, and implement such an agreement was Hassan Vosuq, a prominent politician who believed Iran's interests were best served by a close alliance with Britain.

To agree to appoint Vosuq as prime minister, Ahmad Shah demanded and received from Britain a payment of 15,000 tomans a month (amounting to about £48,000 a year) for as long as he kept Vosuq in office. When the agreement was finalized, to approve the agreement, Ahmad Shah demanded the continuation for life of the subsidy he was receiving from England and additional British guarantees for himself and his dynasty (the British agreed to pay the subsidy for only so long as Vosuq remained prime minister). Meantime, Vosuq and the two cabinet ministers who had negotiated the agreement with Cox asked for an "advance" of £200,000 on the British loan—money they said they needed to win support for the agreement from members of Parliament and other officials. There was no question in the minds of Curzon, Cox, and British officials who agreed to pay this sum that they were being asked for a bribe. In fact, Vosuq shared the "advance" with his two ministers. (When details of the agreement and the bribe money became public, it predictably proved highly unpopular and parliamentary approval impossible to secure. Eventually, a new Iranian government cancelled it in 1921.)[3]

By 1920, feeling was widespread among politically aware Iranians that something fundamental had to be done: Iran needed an army capable of protecting the country's borders and bringing unruly tribes to heel; and it needed a strong central government that would end the chaos, undertake fundamental reforms, revive the economy, and inculcate among the people a sense of national unity and purpose. Members of the political elite met, sometimes openly, sometimes in private, to ponder means of bringing a strong government to office. A number were in touch with British diplomats in Tehran who were thinking along the same lines. Among these was Seyyed Zia ad-Din Tabataba'i, a journalist and political activist with high ambitions. He was on friendly terms with British diplomats in Tehran and often served as intermediary between the legation and Iranian politicians. His newspaper, *Ra'ad*, advocated a range of sweeping reforms. The *Pulad* (Steel) Committee he founded and led brought together intellectuals, reform-minded politicians, and gendarmerie officers for discussions on means to cure the nation's ills. He had big plans and ideas; what he lacked were the means to realize them.

We can only guess at Reza Khan's state of mind at this critical moment in Iran's modern history; but he was certainly touched by these same currents. He had grown contemptuous of the politicians in Tehran who talked endlessly but took no action, and who enriched themselves in office while the soldiers who fought for the country went barefoot. He resented the fact that his own Cossack Brigade was officered by Russians. Judging by his policies when finally in power, we can conclude that he was aware that Iran had fallen behind the West. He later wrote that he found himself "sunk in grief" at prevailing conditions.[4] He was eager to do something for his country; and an unanticipated turn of events gave him the opportunity.

The Russian revolution had broken the link between the Cossack Brigade's Russian officers and the Russian government, allowing the British to achieve their long-sought goal and to rid the brigade of its Russians. The shah agreed to send home the Russian commander and officers of the brigade. The brigade was now effectively in the hands of General Ironside and the British military adviser, Col. C. D. Smythe. Their attention had been drawn to the men under Reza Khan's command. Unlike troops in other detachments, the men were cheery, their training was advanced, and they went about their duties with energy. Reza Khan, too, impressed them: a well-built man, over 6 feet tall, with piercing eyes, self-assured, and with a commanding presence. He appears to have spoken openly to Ironside about his ambitions for Iran. The shah had appointed a feckless royal prince with no military experience as the brigade's commander; but before withdrawing from Iran with his British troops in February 1921, Ironside, with the shah's approval, had placed effective command of the brigade in Reza Khan's hands.[5] Reza Khan was now in control of the only real military force in the country.

The Coup

At a moment when the air was full of rumors of impending change and the country appeared on the edge of a major upheaval, intermediaries brought Seyyed Zia and Reza Khan together: the ambitious political activist and schemer, who had political connections but no power, and the soldier who had few political connections but troops under his command had joined hands. On the night of February 20, 1921, Reza Khan, with Seyyed Zia at his side, marched the Cossacks into the capital and occupied it with virtually no resistance. A thoroughly frightened Ahmad Shah agreed to name Seyyed Zia prime minister and Reza Khan commander of the armed forces, with the title of *Sardar-e Sepah.*

The two men came to office with ideas for sweeping reform—in effect the rejuvenation of Iran: to end corruption, internal divisions, and foreign interference; to create a strong government and army; to revive the economy; and to bring Iran into the modern world. In their first steps, they arrested some twenty prominent notables, in part to squeeze them for money to help finance government operations; they cancelled the still unratified Anglo-Persian Agreement; and they concluded an agreement with the new Soviet government. In exchange for an undertaking not to allow any foreign forces hostile to the Soviet Union to establish military bases on Iranian soil, the Soviet government cancelled all the privileges and concessions (except for the fisheries concession) Tsarist Russia had acquired in Iran and all debts Iran owed to Russia. Seyyed Zia, however, did not survive politically to carry out the rest of the duumvirate's ambitious program. Reza Khan had his own plans, wanted power in his hands alone, and, of the two men, proved to be the firmer of purpose and the more skillful politician. Within three months, he had become war minister and had forced Seyyed Zia into exile; two years later, he was prime minister; and Ahmad Shah, thoroughly cowed by Reza Khan's rising power, left for Europe never to return.

With the shah out of the way, the men around Reza Khan, no doubt with his concurrence, launched a campaign for the declaration of a republic with Reza Khan as president. They were inspired by the example of another military man, Kemal Ataturk in neighboring Turkey, who in 1922 had abolished the Ottoman sultanate, established a republic, and, as president, was energetically transforming his country in a program of modernization, Westernization, and reform. Republicanism and Kemalism, however, did not sit well with Iran's senior clergy. Along with the sultanate, Ataturk had also abolished the Ottoman caliphate; he was not only modernizing but also secularizing his country. Faced with adamant clerical opposition, and after a meeting with the senior clergy in the shrine city of Qum, Reza Khan asked his followers to end all talk of a republic. Yet, Reza Khan was already the undisputed master of Iran; to the political class he had become indispensable for maintaining order and effective government. When he resigned as prime minister in April 1923 and retired to the village of Rudehen outside Tehran, the result, according to the historian, L. P. Elwell-Sutton, "was panic."[6] The Majlis voted overwhelmingly to ask him to return and sent a high-powered delegation to persuade him to do so. In October 1925, the Parliament passed a bill deposing the Qajar dynasty and appointing Reza Khan temporary head of state. In December, a constituent assembly, packed with Reza Khan's supporters, voted to amend the constitution and to vest the monarchy in Reza Shah and his descendants. He was crowned shah in April 1926.

In the two decades that followed the 1921 coup, as military strongman, prime minister, and king, Reza Khan/Reza Shah reshaped Iran in myriad ways. He did not do so alone. He attracted and recruited into his service a number of highly capable men who shared with him the desire to turn Iran into a modern nation-state. The ideas that shaped the extensive reforms that these men carried out were already current among the Westernized intelligentsia, and were echoed in articles in the reformist press and in the programs of the reformist political parties.

In brief, the reformers believed Iran needed to bring into being a strong, well-organized state, a strong army, and a merit-based, modern bureaucracy—to expand commerce, build factories, lift its peasants out of poverty, and put in place a progressive income tax. It needed to educate its children, including girls, and to improve the status of women. Some intellectuals, impressed by the role women played in European societies, advocated for the abolition of the veil. Anti-clericalism—a conviction that the clergy, with their fixation on *shari'a* law, traditionalism, and superstition, constituted a major obstacle to reform—constituted a strong undercurrent in reformist thought. "The corruption existing in Iran is entirely the fault of the clergy," asserted the newspaper, *Rastakhiz*.[7]

Also widespread was the conviction that Iran's maladies were rooted in its tribal, ethnic, sectarian, linguistic, and communal divisions. Iranians were divided into tribes as Turks, Kurds, Arabs, Qashqa'is, and Lurs; each of these groups wore a different headdress and costume; each spoke its own language.

Iranians were most likely to identify themselves by their regional backgrounds, as Isfahanis, Shirazis, or Azarbaijanis, rather than as Iranians. Many spoke a local dialect rather than pure Persian. So went the argument. According to the intellectual and historian, Ahmad Kasravi, such divisions accounted for Iran's backwardness and weakness; and the Constitutional Revolution of 1906 itself was wrecked on the rocks of this fragmentation. "The worst calamity that can befall a nation is disunity … Factionalism is one of the worst maladies afflicting Iran," he wrote.[8] Iran needed to inculcate in its people the same nation-state sentiments that helped create modern Italy, Germany, and Poland, wrote the newspaper *Ayandeh*;[9] Iranians needed to be forged into a nation, and this required the instruction of all Iranians in the Persian language and its history and culture, the eradication of tribal and regional costumes, and the replacement of non-Persian with Persian terms and place names. Deeply nationalistic, the men around Reza Shah were also Westernizers. Iran had fallen behind the advanced nations of Europe; and it had to be transformed, and where appropriate, on the European model. They believed that the state must be the instrument by which Iran could be transformed into a modern country; and once in power, it was through the government—by extending the reach of the state into the furthest corners of the country and even into the private lives of Iranians—that Reza Shah and his lieutenants sought to achieve their goals.

A striking number of the men drawn to Reza Khan and the later Reza Shah had studied in the West; some came from clerical backgrounds but had abandoned clerical studies and family traditions to study abroad; others had played a role in the Constitutional Revolution and now saw an opportunity to realize, through Reza Khan and then Reza Shah, the disappointed hopes of the constitutionalists. That such individuals were drawn to, supported, and served a military man who, from the start, displayed strong authoritarian tendencies is not difficult to explain. By 1920, internal weakness, a failed political system, and disappointed hopes had led many to conclude that Iran needed a strong leader to impose order and overcome obstacles to change and reform. For its regeneration, Iran needed "a revolutionary dictator," according to the newspaper, *Farangistan*. "Our only hope is a Mussolini who can break the influence of the traditional authorities and thus create a modern outlook, a modern people, and a modern nation."[10]

Creating a New Army, a New Administration

Reza Shah's first priority was the army. Immediately after the 1921 coup, he pulled together the Cossack Brigade, the Tehran-based Central Brigade, and what remained of the SPR to begin the process of creating a unified national army. He transferred control of the gendarmerie from the interior ministry to the ministry of war. He took care throughout, as military commander, prime minister, and shah, to ensure that the army was well funded from reliable sources of revenue. To ensure that the government had the revenues to cover military and other expenses, he provided army backing to tax collectors assigned to collect taxes in tribal regions and other tax-resistant, difficult-to-access, areas. He used the military budget to increase the size of the army, purchase armaments abroad, and establish a motorized unit and a small navy and air force. He sent officers for advanced training abroad, primarily to the St. Cyr military academy in France, favored the officer class with better pay and other privileges, and as shah often appointed military officers as provincial governors. By 1941, the ministry of war accounted for some 30 percent of the national budget; and, thanks to the conscription law of 1925 that, with some exceptions, required every young adult to do two years of military service and to serve for several more years in the reserves, the few thousand men under arms in 1921 had grown into an army of over 40,000 by 1925 and over 120,000 toward the end of his reign.

Reza Khan used the army to suppress local political uprisings in Gilan, Azarbaijan, and Khorasan; to tame and disarm the tribes; and to end banditry. The tribes posed a problem for a number of reasons. The tribesmen were armed; the chiefs enjoyed a power base of their own and resisted central government control, taxation, and conscription; and the tribesmen engaged in brigandry, rendering the roads unsafe. Moreover, to the men around Reza Khan, the nomadic way of life appeared outdated and inconsistent with a modern nation-state. Between 1921 and 1925, Reza Khan waged a series of successful campaigns against the Bakhtiari, Qashqai'i, Shahsavan, Lurs, Kurds, Turkomans, and other tribal groups. After 1925, the tribes, except for minor rebellions, no longer posed a serious threat to the government.

Reza Khan launched his most ambitious military campaign against the powerful Shaikh Khaz'al of Mohammerah in the province of Khuzestan.

Khaz'al was virtually autonomous in his province. He resisted paying taxes. Khuzestan was the home of Iran's oil industry, by far the country's largest single source of revenue and of foreign exchange, and also crucial to the British interests. Britain held the majority of shares in the Anglo-Persian Oil Company (APOC). The British government had signed agreements with Khaz'al for the lease of land and the provision of tribesmen to guard oil installations and a separate agreement under which Khaz'al would safeguard British interests and they would protect his primacy in Khuzestan. Conscious of the threat posed by the growing power of the central government, Khaz'al organized a coalition of other tribal chiefs to oppose Reza Khan, urged the absent Ahmad Shah to return from Europe, and sought support and engaged in intrigue with the anti-Reza Khan members of the Majlis. He even suggested annexation of the province of Khuzestan by the government of Iran's neighbor, Iraq.

In November 1925, Reza Khan himself led the military operation to bring Khaz'al to heel, ignoring British urging and pressure to turn back. With Reza Khan at the gates of Khuzestan and realizing that he had exhausted his options, Khaz'al abjectly surrendered, first in a telegram, then in person. He was permitted to return to Khuzestan—but only briefly. In 1925, Reza Khan had Khaz'al arrested, and his vast estates were confiscated. He was brought to Tehran where he lived in comfort, but effectively under house arrest, until he died in 1936.

Reza Khan returned from Khuzestan in triumph; he had tamed the tribes, made the roads safe, and, unlike the politicians, had shown he could take decisions and carry them out. Now, he had taken on a protégé of the British and humbled him, confirming his standing as the most powerful man in Iran. Assumption of the crown soon followed.

With the country largely pacified, Reza Shah and his men turned their attention to the reform of the government administration. They created new ministries and restructured existing ones, defining their responsibilities and the demarcations between them. They reorganized the civil service along European lines. A new law defined civil service ranks, education, and other qualification requirements, pay and retirement benefits, and guidelines for promotions; it called for competitive examinations for entry into the civil service; and classes were later established for the training of civil servants. Provincial government was also thoroughly revamped. The disorderly system of provincial administration under the Qajars was swept away. The country was divided into ten large provinces with clearly defined borders and each administered by governor-general based in a provincial capital. The provinces were subdivided into counties, townships, and districts, each with its own administrative officer down to the village level. Mayors were appointed to the cities and towns; and municipal administrations were created and their responsibilities and revenue sources defined. A national police force was established to maintain order and enforce regulations in urban areas.

The Judiciary, Education, and Women's Emancipation

Judicial reform stretched out over many years, beginning when Reza Khan was prime minister and continuing during his monarchy. Reza Shah's very able minister of justice, Ali-Akbar Davar, a graduate of the Geneva University faculty of law, was the architect of this daunting undertaking. Under his guidance, the ministry of justice was totally revamped. A system of graduated courts was established at the local, county, and provincial levels; a supreme court based in Tehran served as the court of final appeal. Laws were written and codified, resulting in a civil code, a penal code, a commercial code, and other laws, often based on French and Swiss models. In time, the faculty of law at Tehran University trained judges for these courts, and dozens of new judges were appointed to the bench. In the codification of the laws, care was taken not to ruffle clerical sensitivities or to appear to encroach on *shari'a* law. But in reality the judicial system was secularized. Secular judges presided over secular courts and judged cases on the basis of secular laws. An attorney general and his deputies represented the state before the courts. The *shari'a* courts and the clerics who ran them were marginalized, confined to matters of family law—marriage, divorce, and appointment of guardians. In 1932 a new law established a registration office and a nationwide network of public notaries for the registration of contracts, deeds, birth, marriages, and deaths, in effect putting in the hands of the state functions that up to then were in the hands of the clergy.

Reza Shah and his lieutenants devoted considerable attention to education. An attempt was made after the Constitutional Revolution to create a system of secular schools, but with limited success. In 1921, no nationwide system of state schools existed, only few dozen schools that educated a few thousand children. Reza Shah gradually developed a nationwide system of primary and secondary schools, including schools for girls. Curricula, based to a large degree on the French model, were written, uniform textbooks published, and statewide final examinations administered.

By 1941, there were over 280,000 students in some 2,300 primary schools and over 28,000 students in secondary schools. The only teachers' training college in place in Tehran in 1921 expanded to thirty-six such colleges across the country. The Tehran Polytechnic and other technical schools offered an education in the sciences and later in engineering; and an academy of music and an academy of fine arts were later added. In 1936, Tehran University—the country's first—opened its doors to women as well as men, offering instruction in the humanities and the sciences, in law, engineering, and medicine and later in theology, the fine arts, and agriculture. Small numbers of students were sent for specialized training abroad. Schools remained segregated and fewer girls than boys attended school. Nevertheless, in 1940, nearly 5,000 girls received their primary (sixth-grade) school certificates and 451 their secondary school certificates.

Steps to improve the status of women went beyond schooling, building on measures adopted following the Constitutional Revolution and the work of pioneering Iranian women. The aim of the men around Reza Shah was to bring women into the public space alongside men and to make it easier for them to enter the labor force. Women were encouraged to revive women's societies or to establish new ones.

Public spaces such as cafes, restaurants, and hotels were required to allow entry to women as well as men. Girls could join a girl scout organization. Reza Shah encouraged women to enter the workforce in "appropriate" occupations such as teaching, and a small number of women joined the civil service. In 1936, Reza Shah took his boldest step in what was termed the emancipation of Iranian women: the *chador*, the form of Islamic dress common in Iran and which covered women from head to toe, was formally banned. "We must never forget that one-half of the population of our country has not been taken into account, that is to say, one-half of the country's working force has been idle," Reza Shah noted when announcing the new measure.[11] The women of the shah's family had set the example by first appearing in public unveiled; once the law was in force, army officers, then senior and lower-rank civil servants were required to appear in public with their wives unveiled. As common in the government's approach, the abolition of the veil was harshly enforced, and instances of policemen ripping off the *chador* from women who appeared on the street wearing it were not uncommon. Although upper-class women had discreetly begun to abandon the veil and to adopt European dress in the privacy of their own circles, this break with age-old traditions proved difficult for women from traditional backgrounds; and many women chose to remain home rather than appear in public unveiled.

Shaping the Economy and Finances, Remaking Cities, Neglecting Agriculture

Reza Shah also devoted considerable attention to economic development. He launched an ambitious road-building program, the key to facilitating the movement of goods, people, and troops between urban centers. By 1940, there were over 15,000 miles of motorable roads in the country, and transport between large towns and cities, which had in the past required weeks, even months, was reduced to a few days. Reza Shah's most ambitious project was the construction of the trans-Iranian railway—a goal of Iranian Westernizers since the last decades of the nineteenth century. The railway, a remarkable feat of engineering that took over ten years and was completed in 1938, ran from Bandar Shapour on the Persian Gulf in the south to Bandar Shah on the Caspian Sea in the north. It was financed entirely from domestic sources by a tax on sugar and tea (Reza Shah was averse to foreign loans) and carried out by the Swedish engineering firm, Kampsax, with the participation of several European and American engineering firms.

The financial system was badly in need of reform. The American military advisor, Arthur Millspaugh, engaged by the Iranian government in 1922, found the state's finances to be in considerable disorder. Taxes were a hodgepodge of customary survivals, enacted laws, and a miscellany of irregular taxes, tolls, and other levies; the tax rolls on land (the principal source of tax revenue) were out of date, land disputes numerous; tax collection weak and tax evasion widespread.[12] Gradually, some order was imposed on the tax system, a uniform 10 percent tax imposed on land, an income tax enacted, and tax collection improved, although inefficiency and corruption in tax collection remained a problem. Government budgeting was systematized. A major step in overhauling the financial system was taken when a national bank, an aspiration of nationalists since the Constitutional Revolution, was established in 1927. The Bank Melli served both as a commercial bank and as the government's central bank. In another assertion of national sovereignty, it took over from the British-owned Imperial Bank of Persia the issuing of banknotes, and it was made responsible for currency and foreign exchange control and other central bank functions.

As in other areas, the inclination of the shah and his officials relied upon management of the economy by the state. Inevitably, the state managed the business of industrialization. The aim was to make Iran self-sufficient in basic consumer goods. Iranian factories now produced cotton, silk, textiles, cement, tobacco and cigarettes, matches, soap, candles, and some chemicals. State enterprises also invested in tanneries and distilleries, foundries, and electric power plants. Targeted tariffs protected the new industries from competition from cheaper foreign goods; and schoolchildren and troops were required to wear uniforms made of locally produced cloth. In 1931, the government established a foreign trade monopoly—in part a response to Soviet state monopolies–allowing the government more control over foreign trade—and led to state monopolies over the production and the trade in tobacco, textiles, sugar, and cement. Due to limited foreign exchange, importers required licenses for the importation of a variety of goods; exporters were required to exchange a large portion of their foreign currency earnings for rials. Nevertheless, as the economy expanded in the Reza Shah years there also emerged a vigorous private sector engaged in domestic trade, imports and exports, light industry, and retail.

Reza Shah's men devoted much effort to urban renewal. In Tehran and in Isfahan, Shiraz, Tabriz, Mashad, and other cities broad, asphalted avenues suitable for motorized traffic cut through and swept away private homes and the complex mesh of narrow streets and alleys that characterized Iranian cities. Imposing city gates (Tehran had twelve such gates), marking the entrance to a city and its major districts, disappeared; modern-style homes catering to a

Westernized upper middle class rose up in new city districts. In the process, the traditional network of tightly knit *mahalehs* (neighborhoods) and a traditional style of urban living were badly disrupted.

Reza Shah and his government paid far less attention to agriculture and to the condition of the peasants. On Reza Shah's own extensive estates, some experimentation with new and better-managed crops took place; the government established an agricultural bank to finance investment in agriculture, an agricultural college to train agronomists, and a forestry school to train experts in forest management. Agricultural and land policy tended to favor large landowners and led to the consolidation of privately owned estates, often at the expense of the peasantry. The land registration law provided landowners with more security of tenure; and the law on provincial reorganization turned the village headman, or *kadkhoda*, who traditionally represented the interests of the entire village, into the representative of the interests of the landlords. A law enacted in 1937 required landlords to maintain irrigation channels and local roads, and to take steps to improve crops and to better the housing and hygiene of the villagers. But the law remained unenforced. Peasants did benefit, as did landlords, when state monopolies provided a guaranteed market and purchased at fixed prices cotton and other agricultural products; but the general expansion of state control meant the appearance, even at the village level, of a host of government officials who lived off the land, imposed new exactions on the peasantry, and used office for personal benefit. Obligatory military service was an additional hardship on the peasantry. In general, the peasants continued to live in poverty and to be heavily taxed and heavily exploited.

Reza Shah was not content with pacifying the tribes and the great Bakhtiari and Qashqa'i tribal confederations. He sought to strip the tribal chiefs of their power, to end tribal migration, and to transform the pastoral tribesmen into cultivators. A number of tribal leaders were exiled, others executed; the Bakhtiari chief, Sardar Asad, was forced to reside in Tehran. The annual migration from winter to summer quarters—critical to the tribal economy— was halted; and many tribal groups were forced to settle in areas unsuitable for year-round grazing of flocks, with inadequate arrangements, training, and the means to sustain themselves in settled life. Whole groups were relocated, enduring considerable hardship during the ill-planned transfers. According to the historian Ann Lambton, "the tribal policy of Riza Shah, ill-conceived and badly executed, resulted in heavy losses in livestock, the impoverishment of the tribes, and diminution of their numbers."[13] After Reza Shah's abdication, most tribal groups returned to their ancestral grounds and sought to resume their old way of life.

The Assault on the Clergy

During his rise to power, Reza Shah took care not to alienate the clerical community. Following his consultation with Qum's senior clerics and abandoning his brief flirtation with republicanism, he went on a pilgrimage to the Shi'ite shrine cities of Najaf and Karbala as token of his own devotion to Islam. In public statements before and after he became shah, he paid due respect to the centrality of Islam in the life of the country. But Reza Shah was determined to break the standing and influence of the clerical community. The *ulama* represented a rival center of power. They enjoyed support among the masses. They had independent sources of income from their management of religious endowments and the *zakat*, the contributions that believers made to senior members of the clergy and that were used, in part, to support charitable activities, mosques, and students and instructors at religious seminaries. Before the new state schools were established, the clergy exercised a near monopoly over the education of the sons of the families of modest means and the poorer classes. For Reza Shah and his lieutenants, the *ulama*, with their focus on traditional religion, *shari'a* law, and traditional practice, were an obstacle to reform and modernization. Articles in the reformist press at the time reflected this mindset. "The root of our evil is … the clergy," claimed a commentary in one newspaper.[14]

The assault on the influence and authority of the clergy was waged on various fronts. Although some religious instruction took place in the network of primary and secondary schools created by Reza Shah, the curriculum of these schools was essentially secular. The state's new court system, as already noted, applied secular, not *shari'a* law, and even in the narrow jurisdiction left to the clerics over matters of family law, the decisions of the *shari'a* courts required approval by the attorney general. The new network of state-certified notaries public robbed the individual cleric of an important source of income. The 1925 conscription law applied, with narrow exceptions, to seminary students as well as to the general public. The uniform dress code restricted traditional clerical dress—the *aba* and the *'amameh*, or the cloak and the turban—to certified members of the clergy. New laws and regulations required state-mandated examination of seminary students and state-approved curricula at religious seminaries. With Tehran University in place, only graduates of its law school could qualify for judgeships; clerics had to take qualifying exams to continue to serve as judges. Tehran University's school of theology provided a path other than the seminaries for training in the religious sciences. In time, the government sought to take over the administration of religious endowments.

Resistance by the clergy to these encroachments on their traditional prerogatives was for the most part ineffective. Conscription was understandably unpopular with the clergy as well as the general public and led to protests in Isfahan and Shiraz, but these initial disturbances soon died down. Riots in 1929 against the uniform dress code (see below) were short-lived. The senior cleric, Ayatollah Mohammad Taqi Bafqi, was imprisoned for six months and exiled to the shrine of Shah Abdol-Azim outside Tehran, allegedly for discourtesy to female members of the royal family during their visit to a shrine in the city of Qum; and another cleric, Hassan Modarress, one of Reza Shah's boldest and most persistent critics in the Majlis, was in 1928 arrested and exiled to eastern Iran; yet neither incident provoked significant unrest. The major clash between the clergy and the state occurred in 1935 over one aspect of the European dress codes (discussed below).

Forging a Nation—and Dressing It Up

Reza Shah and his men pursued their goal of forging Iranians into one nation by both indirect and direct measures. National conscription brought together all men of military age into one organization to be instructed in common values and inculcated with the ideal of service to country. Schools and the scout organizations sought to imbue young boys and girls with patriotism

and devotion to Iran. Students were taught to take pride in Iran's history—
not the history of Iran under Islam, which was deemphasized, but the history
of Iran in its days of ancient greatness, when under the Achaemenids and
succeeding dynasties, Iran was a great empire and a world power. The massive
remains of the Achaemenid capital at Persepolis were restored, and Persepolis
became a site for Iranians and foreigners to visit and admire. Influenced by the
American art historian, Arthur Upham Pope, Reza Shah took a special interest
in the restoration of Isfahan's historic buildings. He granted Pope permission
to enter and photograph Isfahan's exceptionally fine mosques (a sacred space
normally barred to non-Muslims), and facilitated the work of Pope and his
wife, Phyliss Ackerman, as they collected material for what became Pope's
massive, six-volume, *A Survey of Persian Art from Prehistoric Times to the
Present*. Reza Shah encouraged other European and American archaeologists
in their excavations into Iran's ancient past.

Special honor was accorded to the poet, Ferdowsi, author of the great Persian
epic, the *Shahnameh (Book of Kings)*, an account of Iran's (mostly legendary)
ancient history and heroes, and a literary work as central to the Iranian national
imagination, self-identity, and language as the *Odyssey* is to the Greeks. In 1934,
a millennial congress brought together eighty distinguished European and
Iranian scholars to mark the one thousandth anniversary of Ferdowsi's birth;
and an imposing marble mausoleum, incorporating elements of Achaemenid
architecture, was erected in Tus to memorialize him. The architectural style of
the Achaemenids was incorporated also in the buildings of the national bank
and the headquarters of the national police in Tehran—further reminders
of Iran's past glory. Arabic place names were Iranized: Arabistan became
Khuzestan, Mohammerah became Khorramshahr; the names of all military
ranks and government ministries (of Arabic and non-Iranian origin) were
replaced by Persian terms; and a Persian academy systematically replaced
Arabic words in common use in the written and spoken language with Persian
ones. The names of the calendar months were Persianized. All honorific titles
were abolished and every Iranian was required to adopt a family name and
obtain a national identity card. In 1935, the government asked all foreign
governments to refer to the country as "Iran" rather than "Persia"—in
accordance with Iranian usage and because "Persia" was thought to associate
Iran with the romantic "orient" rather than with modernism. Reza Shah chose

as the name of his dynasty "Pahlavi," the official language of the pre-Islamic Sassanid dynasty (224–651 CE).

These measures of "Persianization" reflected and reinforced the intense nationalism that was characteristic of Reza Shah himself, the men around him, and the period in general. Much to the consternation of European governments but to acclaim at home, and in another bold assertion of national sovereignty, Reza Shah in 1928 abolished the humiliating capitulations: under the Qajars in the nineteenth century Iran had agreed that Europeans in Iran, charged with violations or involved in financial and other legal disputes, would be tried before their own consular courts rather than by Iranian courts. Reza Shah remained sensitive throughout his reign to the treatment in the foreign press of Iran that he deemed disrespectful of Iran's dignity or to his own *amour propre*. Relations with Germany came close to rupture due to an unfavorable article in a German newspaper. He withdrew his envoy and suspended diplomatic relations with the United States when the envoy was stopped and briefly detained for a traffic violation in Washington. In 1936 he broke diplomatic relations with France over a cartoon of Reza Shah in a Paris newspaper, playfully built around the similar French pronunciation of "shah" and "*chat*," the French word for "cat."

The attention that Reza Shah and his men paid to the way Iranians clothed themselves was driven by two goals: to erase tribal, regional, and ethnic distinctions between Iranians as expressed in matters of dress and to smooth the path for modernization—goals aptly described by Houchang Chehabi as "sartorial uniformity" and "sartorial Europeanization."[15] If Iranians dressed alike, so the thinking went, they would feel like members of one community; and if they dressed as did the Europeans they were more likely to behave and think like Europeans and "to capitulate to the advance of Western civilization."[16] In 1927, a cabinet decree required all Iranian men to wear what came to be known as the Pahlavi hat, a head cover that resembled the French peaked kepi. Clerical objections focused on the visor, which would impede (intentionally, cynics thought) the required touching of the forehead to the ground in prayer. This was followed in 1929 by the uniform dress code, which required all men to wear European-style suits, with only members of the clergy and seminary students excepted. In 1935 the European fedora was made mandatory for all men. In matters of dress, as in other areas, Reza Shah and his men sought to free Iran of Western influence, even as they based their reforms on the model of the West.

Resentment was still simmering over the imposition of the Pahlavi hat and the uniform dress code, and the abolition of the veil was sensed to be in the offing. The law requiring adoption of European-style hats proved to be the breaking point, and the clerical reaction was swift. At the Gowharshad mosque in Mashad, home to one of the holiest shrines in Shi'ite Islam, a preacher urged believers to gather at the mosque in protest. The protests grew in scope and numbers. Troops entered the mosque precincts—itself an unprecedented violation of sacred space—and when they failed to disperse the crowds, they opened fire, killing and injuring dozens. To assuage the clerical and public outrage that followed, the custodian of the shrine was tried and executed. But for the clerical community, little else changed.

The modernization project zealously pursued by Reza Shah's men aimed, in essence, at a form of social engineering, at the creation of a new Iranian man. According to the manifesto of the *Iran-e Now* (New Iran) Party, intended by court minister Abdul-Husayn Taymurtash as an all-encompassing government party, Iran under Reza Shah would progress from its present state to "civilization and modernity" and the Iranian people from "lethargy to energy, from individualism to altruism, from prevarication to simple truth, from corruption to rugged honesty."[17] Reza Shah, in his speech at the opening of the Ninth Majlis, called on the deputies to focus on "the moral purification and the education of the public."[18]

Only by an Iron Will

Reza Shah was by temperament an autocrat—a product of his military upbringing and of a conviction that only an iron will and firm control could remold an old, effete ruling class, squabbling politicians, a tradition-bound clergy, a largely uneducated and destitute population, and a country that had failed to keep up with the times into a modern, prosperous Iran that could hold its head high among nations. Adept during his rise to power at working with political parties and politicians and in winning broader popular support, as shah he grew increasingly intolerant of the slow pace of parliamentary politics, criticism or dissent, and any lapse in the rapid progress of his plans and projects. He turned the Majlis into a rubber stamp, strictly controlled elections, and selected many of the "elected" deputies himself. He banned labor unions and arrested student and other political activists, including fifty-three Marxists who were put on trial and, with few exceptions, sentenced to long prison sentences. He suppressed political parties, even those that had supported his rise to power, closed down independent newspapers, and turned the press into an echo chamber for government policy and official views. He instilled fear, even in his own ministers, by his ferocious temper at what he regarded as incompetence or laxness in the performance of duties; he was known to thrash his own ministers when displeased. Sycophancy and adulation of the person of the shah became the norm—the common currency of the press, officials, and parliamentary deputies.

Opponents and men with independent sources of power were excluded from public life or suffered a worse fate. A number of Bakhtiari and Qashqa'i khans were executed; and the Bakhtiari chief, Sardar Asad, at one time Reza Shah's minister of war, died during his obligatory residence in Tehran. The powerful Gilani landowner, Sepahdar-e Tonkaboni, fearing financial ruin at the hands of the state, committed suicide. Reza Shah's attitude toward men to whom he had assigned significant responsibilities could easily turn from trust into gnawing suspicion. Ahmad Qavam, his one-time prime minister and one of Iran's most prominent politicians, fled abroad. Davar, the architect of his financial and judicial reforms, fearing he had incurred Reza Shah's displeasure, committed suicide. Nosrat od-Dowleh Firouz, his minister of finance, was in 1927 charged with financial misconduct and imprisoned.[19]

The fall from grace of Taymourtash, minister of court since the beginning of Reza Shah's reign, was particularly dramatic. Handsome, knowledgeable, and skilled in both politics and diplomacy, fluent in several languages, Taymourtash became Reza Shah's most trusted lieutenant and was considered by both the Iranian elite and foreign diplomats as the second most powerful man in Iran. The shah relied on him to oversee most of the business of government. Although not a member of the cabinet, he directed cabinet meetings and discussions, he negotiated with foreign embassies, and he was responsible for major political initiatives. Perhaps precisely because of such prominence, or because of his allegedly pro-Russian inclinations (Taymourtash had trained at a Russian military academy), or because enemies and rivals planted suspicions in Reza Shah's mind and circulated rumors that Taymourtash aimed to establish and head a republic after Reza Shah's death, he was arrested on charges of corruption 1933, incarcerated under harsh conditions, and, like Firouz, died in prison. The belief that Reza Shah was personally responsible for the deaths of Taymourtash, Firouz, Sardar Asad, and Shaikh Khaz'al has persisted.

There were others who incurred Reza Shah's displeasure and whose lives were also ended. The landowner and senior government official, Abdol-Husayn Diba, died in prison while awaiting trial. The poet, Farrokhi, died in a prison hospital. Ali Dashti, a Majlis deputy, writer, and journalist, was stripped of his parliamentary immunity and sent to an insane asylum. The Jewish deputy, Samuel Haim, was executed, allegedly for encouraging his Jewish compatriots to emigrate to Palestine. The Zoroastrian deputy, Arbab Kaykhosrow, was gunned down on a Tehran street, presumably because his son in Nazi Germany had been broadcasting items critical of Iran. Modarress, too, died in exile in suspicious circumstances.[20]

Foreign Policy in a Time of War

Reza Shah's foreign policy prioritized relations with Iran's immediate neighbors, Turkey and Afghanistan, and the two great powers at Iran's door, the Soviet Union to the north and Britain in the Persian Gulf, and also with major trading partners, particularly Germany. The 1937 Saadabad Pact brought together Iran, Iraq, Turkey, and Afghanistan in a nonaggression treaty. Reza Shah paid his only state visit to Turkey; as modernizing military men and nationalists, the shah and Ataturk shared much in common. He cultivated good relations with both USSR and England, although there was friction at times over the terms of trade, particularly with the USSR; both countries remained significant trading partners, and Iran relied on the overland route through the Soviet Union for imports and exports to and from Europe.

Considering the terms of Iran's agreement with the APOC unfair, and pressing for a larger share of APOC profits to finance his many projects, Reza Shah cancelled the agreement in 1932. Protracted negotiations led to a new agreement in 1933: the APOC agreed to increase royalty payments to Iran from

16 to 20 percent of profits and to train more Iranians for senior administrative positions; and Iran agreed to extend the life of the agreement, due to expire in 1961, for another thirty-two years to 1993. The lengthy extension came in for much criticism after Reza Shah's abdication. Reza Shah, sensitive to the dominant and intrusive role of Russia and Britain in Iran in the nineteenth and the early twentieth centuries, took care to engage other countries in Iran's development. Foreign advisers tended to come from countries other than these two great powers. In the economic sphere, Germany's role was prominent. By 1940, Germany ranked first among Iran's trading partners; and German firms and technicians were involved in a large number of industrial projects, in installing machinery and factories, and in training Iranians to run them.

While Reza Shah admired Germany for its strict discipline, firm leadership, hardworking people, and industrial prowess, there is little indication that Reza Shah comprehended in any depth the malign nature of the fascist state Hitler had constructed in Germany; nor that he grasped fully the life-and-death issues at stake for England and its allies when the Second World War broke out and as Hitler overran Europe and occupied France. He had tried to meet halfway British and Soviet demands by expelling some of the Germans, but not enough to satisfy the allies. Besides Britain and the Soviet Union were never fully open with Reza Shah. Pressing for the expulsion of the Germans, they did not tell Reza Shah, or his prime minister and foreign minister, that, once Hitler invaded the Soviet Union, free access to Iran's overland routes and railway to supply the Soviet Union had become vital to the Allied war effort. Reza Shah's purpose was to keep Iran out of the war, to maintain insofar as possible normal trade relations with countries on both sides of the conflict, and to prevent interruption of the numerous industrial and other projects in which they were involved. He did not foresee that the inexorable logic of war would upend all his plans and calculations, that his country would be invaded and occupied, and that he would lose his throne and live out the rest of his life in exile.

2

Britain and the Abdication of Reza Shah

In August 1941, on the eve of the Anglo-Russian invasion of Iran in the Second World War, the British minister to Tehran, Reader Bullard, urged his government to dissociate itself from Reza Shah; and he directly touched on the desirability of the removal of the shah from power. "I fear nothing but the fall of the Shah will set us free from identification with his misdeeds,"[1] he wrote. In the weeks following the Anglo-Soviet occupation of Iran, Bullard would repeatedly press for, and ultimately help determine, the British decision to force Reza Shah to abdicate and to go into exile. Returning to the subject two weeks after Russian and British troops had entered Iran, Bullard described Reza Shah as behaving like the "greedy ignorant savage his people think him," and reported that his entire legation staff, without exception, "have got to the point when we believe the shah is in fact incorrigible."[2]

Yet, this was not always Bullard's view of the British relationship with the Iranian ruler. Only twenty months earlier, when he presented his credentials as England's new minister to the shah's court, he was pleased to report to the foreign secretary, Lord Halifax, that the normally gloomy shah was "good humored and even genial" during the meeting; and he wrote that he regarded it "as one of my most urgent duties" to convince the Iranian government that, despite war conditions, Britain was doing its best to meet Iran's requirements in terms of rails, aircraft, and other materials.[3] In the year and more that followed, Bullard worked hard to accommodate the shah in three related areas: materials Iran wished to purchase from Britain; British credits to help pay for these goods; and an exemption from the British Reprisals Order in Council of November 1939, which authorized the seizure of goods of German origin on the high seas, even on neutral ships.

Like Bullard, the British government wished to remain on good terms with Reza Shah. Iran's oil was crucial to the British war effort. England had no desire to push Reza Shah into the arms of the Germans, who already had a considerable presence in Iran. For these reasons, the British agreed to exempt certain categories of goods purchased by Iran from Germany from the Order in Council. Additionally, as Bullard reminded the Foreign Office on more than one occasion, the policy of neutrality adopted by the shah well suited Britain's war interests. "As the Shah keeps order and maintains neutrality, his continuance in office during the war probably suits us better than any practicable alternative," he wrote in May 1941.[4] Two months later, discussing British press reporting on Iran, he cabled home, "I suggest the policy for us is to advertise and maintain the Shah's policy of neutrality with which you were not dissatisfied during the Iraqi troubles."[5] The Foreign Office largely shared this view.[6]

But difficulties arose over the interpretation of the exemption from the Order in Council Britain was allowing Iran and also over the arms, rails, locomotives, and other goods the British had promised Iran but then found themselves unable to deliver. As such obstacles arose, it was Bullard who took the lead in urging his government to find ways of overcoming them.

Earlier, when war broke out in September 1939, Iran had declared its neutrality. Iran had trade relations with all the chief belligerents. The shah's ambitious economic projects, which he did not wish interrupted, relied on this trade; and, given Iran's experience in the First World War when it became a battleground for the belligerents, he was determined to keep Iran out of the war. Iran's industrial development was particularly dependent on German machinery, technical support, and technicians. German machinery for Iranian plants, including blast furnaces for an iron smelting foundry, was still sitting in Germany or in Trieste, awaiting onward shipment to Iran on neutral vessels. Arms ordered in Czechoslovakia had yet to be shipped to Iran. Before releasing these materials, the Germans demanded assurances they would not fall into British hands; and Iran was anxious that the Order in Council not result in the seizure of these goods. As a special consideration, as noted, the British government decided to exempt German goods, including armaments, which were ordered and paid for by Iran prior to the outbreak of hostilities. This exemption was later extended to include goods ordered and paid for prior to the date of the Order in Council, then to all Iran-bound German goods in Trieste as of May 10, 1940.[7] But difficulties persisted. The

Iranians proved unwilling or unable to submit the detailed paperwork for each shipment demanded by the British. They had placed orders in Germany after the British embargo on German trade and wished these to be exempted as well. Under the Iran–Germany clearing agreement, Iran had piled up a surplus of 40 million Reichmarks it wanted to use for the purchase of German goods, a request Bullard thought reasonable. The Iranian minister in London argued persuasively that permits issued by Britain for a silk-stocking factory or the smelting foundry served little purpose if they permitted the delivery of some, not all, of the required machinery.[8]

In addition, under an agreement signed in February 1940,[9] the British had agreed to extend to Iran a £5 million credit for the purchase of British goods. Here, too, the British appeared ready to be accommodating, for example, dropping the requirement that the credit agreement be approved by the Iranian Parliament. Iran initially intended to use the entire £5 million credit for the purchase of armaments, particularly aircraft. However, given war conditions, England decided it could not supply the bombers and fighter aircraft Iran desired; nor could it afford the railroad cars, rails, and locomotives that Iran requested as a substitute. London also interpreted the terms of the credit as not applicable to the purchase of nonmilitary material, such as cement, or for purchases in India where locomotives and cement were available.

Bullard, in Tehran, was keenly sensitive to the need to retain the shah's goodwill, especially in light of the effectiveness of German war propaganda and early German victories, and German ability to continue to supply Iran with the goods it needed. Repeatedly, it was Bullard who argued Iran's case with his government. When difficulties arose regarding permits for Iranian goods at Trieste, Bullard urged accommodating Iran, especially in the case of the blast furnaces: "Any concession His Majesty's Government will be able to make about this material," he wrote, would bolster Britain's standing in Tehran.[10] When the foreign secretary Lord Halifax telegraphed Bullard that the credits could not be used for nonwar materials, such as rails and cement, Bullard immediately telegraphed back: "If I were obliged to convey to His Majesty that not only we are not in a position to supply war material but also that he may not use the credit for commercial purchases in the United Kingdom, British interests and prestige would suffer a very severe blow."[11] A few days later, in reply to a Foreign Office query, he cabled, "I can only urge the most liberal interpretation of the Credit Agreement, e.g., to cover cement and locomotives and the most generous treatment possible of German goods consigned to Iran via Trieste."[12]

Unable to secure the arms and other goods he wanted from England, a piqued Reza Shah cancelled the credit agreement in June 1940. Bullard, while noting that the shah's grievances against England were unjustified, added, "It would have paid us handsomely to be more accommodating, especially as to cement and locomotives."[13] The Government of India offered to supply rails that Britain's designated steel company could no longer spare but, much to the shah's displeasure, only at a higher price. Again, it was Bullard who sought a way out, suggesting, by way of a compromise, that half the rails be supplied at a lower price. His proposal, he wrote, was most important to please Reza Shah and added, "I ... beg that it be given earnest and urgent consideration."[14]

The German Presence in Iran

The large German presence in Iran, especially in such strategic fields as communications, the railways, and broadcasting, was of considerable concern to both Bullard and the Foreign Office. The new German ambassador, Erwin Ettel, was energetic in organizing the German community in Iran along Nazi party lines; and the British believed, though they could not prove, that many Germans in Iran were collecting intelligence and constituted a potential fifth column. German propaganda, Bullard noted, was more effective than England's. The British feared possible sabotage of the oil installations and communications lines, or an attempt to install a pro-German government in Tehran. Concern over the German presence intensified with the Rashid Ali coup in Iraq in May 1941, when pro-German Iraqi officers seized power, caused the flight of the young king and the pro-British regent, threatened the British military presence, and sought German military assistance. The British landed troops, and by the end of May had routed the Rashid Ali forces and returned the king and the regent to power. But the threat to British interests had for a moment appeared grave, raising fears of a similar coup attempt by pro-German military officers in Iran. Bullard, for example, thought the Germans might try to seize the right bank of the Iran–Iraq waterway, the Shatt al-Arab, or bring to power a pro-German government in Tehran and deprive Britain of access to Iranian oil.[15]

Acting on instructions from Halifax and then Anthony Eden, his successor as foreign secretary, Bullard repeatedly urged the Iranians to reduce the number of Germans in Iran and attempted, as Eden put it, "jolting them out of their apparent complacency." The German presence in all small countries meant intrigue, fifth column activities and attempts to overthrow legitimate governments, the British argued. The disaster that befell Iraq could befall Iran, where the Germans might attempt to install a pro-German government or overthrow the regime. Rather than offer Iran protection against Russia as the Iranian government hoped, the Germans would cede northern Iran to the Russians in exchange for a free hand in Europe. Germany's ally, Italy, coveted Muslim territory and might attack the Persian oilfields.[16]

The Iranian government did take some steps in response to British urgings. They recalled to Tehran all Germans from Khuzestan to guard against possible sabotage of oil installations, sent a number of Germans home, and kept close watch on other members of the German community. They warned all foreign residents against engaging in political activity not in keeping with Iran's neutrality policy; and they ensured that press reports did not favor either side in the conflict. They imposed restrictions on visas issued by Iran's embassies abroad.[17]

Yet, these measures proved insufficient to allay British concerns. Bullard and senior Foreign Office officials well understood the reasons for the shah's reluctance to move more forcefully against the Germans: Germany supplied almost all of the machinery for Iran's industries and was the principal purchaser of Iranian raw materials and goods. German technicians were essential for the installation of machinery and plant in numerous projects around the country. The shah had purchased the bulk of his weaponry from Czechoslovakia, deliberately avoiding reliance on Germany; but the German occupation of Czechoslovakia in March 1939 meant these arms must come from German-controlled firms as well. The Germans, the Iranians told the British, would view any demand for the large-scale departure of their nationals as a violation of Iranian neutrality and would retaliate. The Iranians were not convinced the Germans would lose the war.[18] Bullard on one occasion argued for a full hour with Iranian premier on Iran's need to reduce the numbers of Germans but, he reported, "I was unable to shake the prime minister."[19] These efforts continued, even though the consensus in the Foreign Office was that, pleadings and warnings aside, there was little further they could do. "The Iranian Government … do not take our warnings to heart," minuted A. V. Coverley-Price at the Foreign Office. It is "useless" to expect the Iranian government to send home a significant number of Germans, Bullard concluded.[20]

Bullard did not anywhere suggest, as did some subsequent accounts, that Reza Shah was pro-German and an admirer of Hitler, and no such blunt assertion is made in the available British records. Bullard's evaluation of Iranian attitudes was far more nuanced. Iranian sentiment, Bullard noted, tended to fluctuate with the fortunes of the belligerents on the battlefield. Fearing Soviet territorial ambitions and believing Germany would protect Iran against Russia, official circles initially expected and hoped for a German victory, he wrote, but "it could not be fairly said they showed pro-German feelings as a whole."[21] Following the Molotov–Ribbentrop pact, however, Iranian trust in Germany faded; Iranians feared Germany had ceded Iran to Russia. Public opinion was strongly pro-German, Bullard wrote, but the official attitude was not. Younger army officers, the Legation reported, tended to be pro-German; but Bullard also took note of the Iranian government's "desire to be conciliatory" and its "surprising promptitude" in responding to various British requests.[22] Regarding Reza Shah, he wrote that "it is certain that the Shah's sympathies, were he to express them, would be found to be more in favor of the Allies than of Germany."[23] After seeing the prime minister and the foreign minister on the German issue in late July, accompanied by his Soviet colleague, he cabled home that "we agree that they are in general well disposed—an opinion shared by all my Allied colleagues and by the American Minister."[24]

Snatching at Straws

In its unsuccessful attempts to persuade the shah to reduce significantly the German presence, the Foreign Office sometimes appeared to be grasping at straws. It launched a quixotic search for someone who could influence the shah; it considered offering Reza Shah "a bribe" in the form of a substantial sum of money; and, briefly, it considered doing away with the Pahlavi monarchy altogether.

The search for someone who might influence Reza Shah was triggered by a chance letter to Henry Hopkinson at the Foreign Office,[25] suggesting individuals the Foreign Office might contact "before it is too late." The letter was from a friend of Hopkinson's, apparently with business interests in Iran. The names he proposed were Lord General Ironside, members of the family of Ernest Perron in Switzerland, and Freya Stark. Ironside, as already noted, had served as the commander of British forces in western Iran near the end of the First World War. He knew and had worked closely with Reza Shah before he rose to power and became the king, and when, as Reza Khan, he was an officer in the Iranian Cossack Brigade. Perron, the son of the groundskeeper at the school the Iranian crown prince Mohammad Reza had attended in Switzerland, had been befriended by the crown prince, and was now attached to the royal court in Tehran. Freya Stark, the traveler and author, was working for the British Ministry of Information in the Middle East during the war and was presumed to have good connections in the Egyptian royal court. Where Stark was concerned, the improbable suggestion of Hopkinson's correspondent was this: Iran's crown prince was married to Princess Fawzia, the sister of Egypt's King Farouq. Stark, it was suggested, could work on the "female connections" of Fawzia in the Egyptian royal family to persuade Fawzia to intercede with her husband who, in turn, would intercede with Reza Shah.

The letter to Hopkinson set off a flurry of correspondence by the Foreign Office. Alexander Cadogan, the permanent undersecretary, wrote to Ironside, asking if he would write privately to Reza Shah, given that "the Shah has for some years become more and more difficult to get to."[26] Cables were sent to the British ambassador in Switzerland, David Kelly, asking him, "with great discretion," to enquire whether the family of Perron, in Coppet, near Lake Geneva, could be used "to instill into the Shah [the] belief in our ultimate victory and to make him realize the dangerous nature of German activities in Iran."[27] A cable was sent to Sir Miles Lampson, the British ambassador in Cairo, suggesting getting to Reza Shah through Princess Fawzia, by way of the women of the Egyptian court.[28]

All these initiatives came to naught. Ironside in effect turned Cadogan down, writing that his correspondence with Reza Shah "just drifted away," some ten years earlier. Kelly's enquiry regarding the Perron family also yielded no fruit.[29] From Cairo, Lampson cabled that it would be impractical to influence the shah through the women of the royal court. Princess Fawzia, he wrote, exercises little influence on her husband, much less on the shah; her family in Egypt would be unwilling intercede with her; and all her Egyptian attendants were long ago sent home by Reza Shah.[30] Stark, who was in Baghdad, came up with the fanciful idea of going to Tehran to consult with Bullard "as to the possibility of engineering the employment of a carefully selected English maid or nurse in the Crown Princess's palace." But Stark did not go to Tehran at the time, and as Lampson observed, Reza Shah was unlikely to allow an Englishwoman into Fawzia's household.

Operation Barbarossa, the German invasion of Russia on July 20, 1941, dramatically altered Britain's calculus on Iran. British officials had little confidence that Russian forces would stop the Germans, and once German forces swept through the Caucasus, the British position in Iran and access to Iranian oil would be seriously threatened.[31] The Soviet Union was now an ally, and the Russians proved even more concerned than the British over German fifth column activities along their long border with Iran and sabotage of the Baku oilfields. Since shipping by the northern sea routes was subject to attack and virtually impossible in winter, access to the overland route through Iran to supply a hard-pressed Russia suddenly loomed large. Although they did not publicly say so, the British recognized that the use of the Iranian route would be incompatible with Iranian neutrality. Within days of Operation Barbarossa, Britain and Russia began to coordinate plans across a wide front, including in Iran. In July and August, they presented parallel notes to the Iranian government, calling for the severe reduction of Germans in Iran; the second, on the Russian side, came close to an ultimatum, although the British carefully avoided the language.

From the start of the Anglo-Soviet coordination on Iran, Eden was convinced that to be effective, pressure on Iran had to be backed by the threat of force; but even as military preparations proceeded, he continued to hope force would not be necessary.[32] However, even though the Iranian government said it was acting to send Germans home, Iran failed adequately to satisfy

Anglo-Soviet demands regarding the Germans, and by late August the die was cast. Russian and British forces crossed into Iran early on the morning of August 25, the Russians from the north, the British from the south and east, and rapidly occupied large parts of the country.

Bullard and Lambton: The Case for Unseating Reza Shah

It is in this context that we must now consider the post-invasion events that led to the decision to force Reza Shah from the throne, a decision in which Bullard played a central role. By the end of his first year in Iran, Bullard's view of Reza Shah and Britain's relationship with the Iranian monarch had begun to alter. "As he ages, he becomes more greedy, more arrogant and remote, and more unpopular," he wrote of the shah early in 1941.[33] He called attention to the burden of indirect taxation on the poor, the scarcity of bread, the high cost of basic foods, and Reza Shah's propensity to amass property by pressuring owners to sell at "ruinously low prices." He suggested that "the chances that the Pahlavi dynasty will maintain itself seem small." Bullard was hardly pleased, even found it "humiliating" and called it "blackmail," when Reza Shah took advantage of a Britain hard-pressed by war to secure from the Anglo-Iranian Oil Company a large cash payment, and secured from the British government the right to convert £6 million (from oil revenues) into scarce US dollars over a two-year period.[34] From Bullard's perspective, England was engaged in a life-and-death struggle with Germany; the outcome of a fateful encounter between freedom and totalitarianism hung in the balance. He was understandably discomfited that all this mattered little to the Iranians. Received by the crown prince, Mohammad Reza, shortly after presenting his credentials to the shah, Bullard noted with barely disguised irony that "His Imperial Highness did not hide his opinion that the war was a nuisance for Iran" and seemed to think peace would have been preserved if only Danzig had been ceded to Germany—views, Bullard thought, that could only come from the shah.[35] Iranians vulnerable themselves, nevertheless, admired power and seemed to care little when Germany overran Holland and Belgium, Bullard noted. Above all, Bullard's view of Britain's relationship with Reza Shah was shaped by a growing belief that Iranians tended to see Reza Shah as a creature of the British and that this close association in the Iranian mind between England and an unpopular ruler was highly detrimental to Britain's interests.

A memo drawn up by Bullard's press attaché, Ann Lambton, in the spring of 1941, shortly after the Rashid Ali coup in Iraq, provides insight into Bullard's thinking. Lambton considered in her memo the likely response of Iranians to German (or Russian) intervention in Iran. She concluded that the vast majority of Iranians would welcome it. She noted that there was in Iran a minority who were pro-German "by conviction"; a pro-British minority that would regret but not oppose a German intervention; a small minority whose interests were tied up with the regime and who desired no change; "and the vast majority who hate the Shah and consistently attribute his sins to the British Government ... To such people even the spread of war to Iran seems preferable to the continuation of the present regime ... indeed, they conceive that as the only way in which the removal of the Shah can be secured."[36] Most Iranians, she wrote, believed that British intervention would only perpetuate the shah's rule, while German intervention might rid them of it. They would not, therefore, resist German or Russian intervention: "They hate the Shah, and so why, they ask, should they fight to perpetuate his rule?" Lambton then posed what became a critical question for the British:

> It would appear that it is now time to consider our policy towards the Shah in the event of a German or Russian occupation of Northern Iran, which can no longer be regarded merely as a remote possibility. Should we in that case give our blessing and support to a Government set up, say, in Fars or Khuzistan, under the aegis of the Shah or give him refuge in some British vessel in the Persian Gulf, with promise of restoration? Such a policy would, it seems to me, be fatal. If we did so, we should confirm the population in their belief that the Shah was our puppet and in their dislike of us for that reason, and convince them even more firmly that their only hope lies with the Germans.[37]

Bullard considered this memorandum sufficiently important to send copies to the Ministry of Information, the Political Intelligence Department of the Foreign Office, the secretary of state for India, the Middle East Intelligence Center in Cairo, and the British ambassadors in Ankara, Baghdad, and Moscow. "Public opinion in Iran," he wrote, in his cover letter endorsing Lambton's views, "is almost solidly against the Shah and almost as solidly persuaded that the Shah would not be on the throne were it not for the British." The Germans were already fomenting trouble in Iraq, Syria, and Palestine; therefore, the attitude the British government should adopt if a movement emerged to drive the shah from the country or the capital was of "great urgency."[38]

Over the coming months, Bullard's dispatches repeatedly echoed the points raised by Lambton's memo: that Reza Shah was universally and intensely disliked; in the popular mind, Britain brought the shah to power and sustained him in office and was for this reason blamed for his misdeeds; the Iranians would welcome a German intrusion; a popular movement against the shah could not be ruled out; the shah might flee his capital and seek British protection in the south; and the only way for Britain to gain some credibility with the Iranian people was to distance itself from the shah. With the Anglo-Soviet occupation of Iran imminent and then a reality, Bullard went a step further, concluding that the retention of the shah on the throne was detrimental to England's interests and that he must be driven out. Bullard's views on Reza Shah's unpopularity gained traction in the Foreign Office; but his insistence that Reza Shah must go initially did not, except with the Government of India. Eden, Middle East hands at the Foreign Office, and Churchill himself resisted Bullard's suggestion that the shah must be removed from power. In the third week of the occupation, however, Bullard's reporting, developments on the ground, and the exigencies of war led to a change. Eden, and the British government itself, concluded Reza Shah had to go.

Bullard's hardened attitude toward Reza Shah is evident in his dispatches. A week after forwarding the Lambton memo, and alarmed by German successes in Iraq, he cabled home that general discontent provided ground for German intrigue and added, "The Shah is object of almost universal execration and we also as his supposed supporters." If the shah were forced from the capital, he would seek British protection in the oil area or elsewhere. "In that case we should I think avoid any action which might be represented as supporting his cause and contemplating his return."[39] Reacting to a suggestion that BBC broadcasts to Iran should alert Iranians to the danger of a German-inspired coup in Iran, Bullard responded that such a warning would be effective only with the shah since most people in Iran would welcome a revolution.[40] Bullard objected on the same grounds to a suggestion put to him by Eden in early August to offer the shah a bribe to expel the Germans.

The idea of using financial incentives to win over Reza Shah was first mooted in late June by C. V. Coverley Price, one of the Foreign Office officials dealing with Iran. It might be possible, he wrote, "to exploit the Shah's greed by offering him, in return for the expulsion of the Germans, a fat bribe, e.g. £6 million or £10 million and, say, 60 aircraft."[41] Eden picked up on this unconventional suggestion in early August, following the German invasion of Russia, and even as Britain and the Soviet Union began considering military action in Iran. On August 4, he took to the War Cabinet a proposal to offer Iran a financial inducement for compliance, perhaps by doubling the royalty paid by the Anglo-Iranian Oil Company to the Iranian government.[42] Three days later, he cabled Bullard that he was proposing to accompany the tough new note on the German issue that Britain and Russia were about to hand to Iran with an offer to help find British and neutral technicians to replace any Germans who were sent away. He also proposed "a substantial lump sum payment," either as an increase in oil revenues or as "a personal subsidy to the Shah, if that could be arranged."[43]

Bullard strongly objected in two successive cables: "Help given to the Shah," he wrote, "would strengthen his position and on the other hand confirm the allegations that we support him against the popular will and that the main object of the occupation (if carried out) is to prolong his reign." He then touched on two points he would pursue intently in the days that followed: the need for the shah to transfer his vast wealth to the Iranian people and the possible deposing of Reza Shah. Britain, he said, "should use this opportunity to secure the transfer to the State of most or all vast possessions such as land, factories and hotels which the Shah has amassed"; and, since the shah would not agree, "the question of a change of rule must therefore be contemplated."[44] Faced with Bullard's objections, Eden reluctantly dropped the idea of "a secret bribe," even though he did ask Bullard to reconsider or at least to consider a financial offer that would not benefit the shah personally but would allow the Iranian government to meet British wishes.[45] Bullard remained adamant. "So long as the Shah remains in power, no payment made to him will benefit the public," he wrote.[46] Since the Exchequer also proved cool to the proposal on practical and financial grounds—the shah had little use for sterling and Britain's dollar and gold reserves were already much reduced—Eden dropped the idea of a financial inducement.[47]

Eden and Churchill: Forcing Abdication

Bullard's initial recommendation, in his August 25 cable, that Britain dissociate itself from (in effect, depose) Reza Shah had met with a negative response from Eden and his Middle East staff at the Foreign Office. "I think our interests will be best served by continuing to deal with the Shah, at any rate for the present. It is clearly in the Shah's own interest to lead his country into cooperation with us," Eden wrote in reply.[48] This was also Churchill's view. "I was glad to gather from you last night that no attack on person of the Shah is contemplated at present," he wrote in a note to Eden.[49] In Cairo, the ambassador, Miles Lampson, acting on a cable from Eden, told the Egyptian prime minister that "Her Majesty's Government had no desire to see the [Pahlavi] dynasty overthrown."[50] Bullard's suggestion that the shah be required to give up some or all of his wealth had also little immediate support at the Foreign Office.[51] Bullard, however, persisted, decrying any cooperation with Reza Shah: "We must be extremely careful," he wrote. "It would be difficult to exaggerate his unpopularity … co-operation with him means supporting him i.e. doing exactly what the people of Persia have always accused us of doing."[52]

The back-and-forth between Bullard and the Foreign Office continued for several more days. Bullard was reinforced in his convictions by fast-moving developments in Iran. The government in office at the moment of the invasion had resigned; and Reza Shah had named as prime minister Mohammad Ali Foroughi, a highly respected scholar and statesman with a reputation for honesty, moderation, and respect for the constitution. Bullard held Foroughi in high regard and felt he and his cabinet officers were cooperating with the British to resolve problems arising out of the occupation. However, the Iranian army had collapsed under the impact of the invasion; central authority was shaken. Long pent-up frustrations with the shah and the government began to be articulated openly. Rumors on August 30 of the shah's impending departure for Isfahan (and his possible abdication), along with a discussion of constitutional government on Tehran radio (probably inspired by Foroughi), further emboldened the shah's critics. The shah, however, did not leave for Isfahan. Bullard reported that people's hopes that he had abdicated were disappointed and "now all is despair again." Britain's popularity had initially risen due to the good behavior of the British occupiers and due to the invasion, which had shaken the shah's rule; but now "the tide has turned strongly against us because the Shah is behaving as before" and because people believe he remained in power due to British support. Bullard was receiving "messages of despair and indignation from all sides" on this account. "We really must show some sympathy with popular opinion in Persia or the weight of hostility to us will clog all our efforts," he wrote.[53]

Eden did act on one of Bullard's suggestions. He ordered, cautiously, as a means "of encouraging our friends among the Persians," BBC Persian-language broadcasts from London and Delhi promoting the idea of constitutional and accountable government; and a call for reform as a means of winning popular support for Britain became embedded in the British policy. However, Eden was not prepared to go further than he had and to attack the shah directly in broadcasts, at least not yet. While the British government appreciated the risk of alienating Iranian goodwill by cooperating with the shah and appearing to support "his tyrannical rule," Eden cabled Bullard,

> At the same time, it was not clear to His Majesty's Government that the time had come for them to take any concrete action. They did not feel able, for example, to take the line that they would only enter into negotiations with the Shah's Government if His Majesty would hand over some of his private property to the Persian State. Nor are His Majesty's Government yet satisfied (although they remain open to conviction on this point) that it would be wise for them openly to turn against the Shah so long as there is a reasonable possibility of his carrying out our essential requirements.[54]

In a subsequent cable, Eden wrote to Bullard: "We have neither the wish nor the intention to prop up the Shah and thus bring his unpopularity upon ourselves." But Eden wanted to be sure that the shah's departure would not lead to disorder and breakdown, and that a post-Reza Shah government would be capable of meeting Britain's needs.[55] Over the next two weeks, three factors swung Eden and the government over to Bullard's view.

First, Bullard continued to report rising popular sentiment against the shah. Three ministers had sent him a message that shah was impossible. At a meeting on September 8, Prime Minister Foroughi informed Bullard that the Iranian Parliament intended to introduce reform measures, but that "the Shah will obstruct and wait for revenge," and that he must go, if there was to be any change. Foroughi knew that the shah was unpopular, but "he has been astounded at the flood of hatred directed against him from everywhere." Bullard also took care to address Eden's concerns regarding the succession: the crown prince would be a constitutional monarch with little power; Foroughi could work with him; and the prime minister and his cabinet, even with Reza Shah still on the throne, had shown strength in accepting the Allies' heavy terms. Bullard urged the intensification of anti-shah propaganda: "Our broadcasts are eagerly awaited and it is time to speak out."[56] This time, in an important shift, the Foreign Office authorized the BBC to broadcast in its Persian-language service direct and escalating criticism of Reza Shah: for the forcible acquisition of land and forced labor on his properties; suppressing the press and manipulating elections; unlawful arrests and executions; government oppression and the prevailing poverty; personal enrichment at public expense; and more.[57] Three days of intensive broadcasts followed. The materials for the broadcasts had been prepared by the press attaché in Tehran, Ann Lambton. Her biographer subsequently ascribed Reza Shah's decision to abdicate largely to these broadcasts: "It was a masterstroke, unexpected and devastating in its consequence," he wrote. He quoted Lambton herself, not a person given to hyperbole, as remarking, "Never, I suppose, have the BBC had such a success, for it was almost entirely due to the Persian broadcasts from London that it happened."[58] Bullard, too, indirectly linked the abdication to the broadcasts.[59]

Second, Bullard and the Foreign Office increasingly felt that the Foroughi government's good intentions notwithstanding, Reza Shah was resisting and would continue to obstruct cooperation with the Allies. On September 9, the Iranian government had reluctantly acceded to Allied demands that it shut down the embassy of Germany and of those of its allies, Italy, Romania, and Hungary, and that it round up and hand over to the British and Russians all German and Italian nationals, except diplomatic staff. But the work went very slowly. By September 14, only eighty Germans had been handed over; the German ambassador was apparently continuing to conduct diplomatic business; and the legations of the Axis powers had not yet been shut down. The British concluded that Reza Shah, "working hand in glove with the Germans," was to blame.[60]

This impression that Reza Shah would stand in the way of Allied aims was reinforced by a September 10 editorial in *Ettelaat*, the country's largest and most important newspaper, widely regarded as the official organ of the state. The editorial regretted the violation of Iranian neutrality by the Allies and the need to close the German, Italian, Hungarian, and Romanian embassies. It went on to assert that Iran would maintain its legations in these countries and continue political relations with the four governments.[61] The editorial did serious damage to Reza Shah's standing with the Allies. Bullard was convinced (and he confirmed with the prime minister) that the editorial was inspired by the royal court. He discussed the editorial with his Soviet colleague; Eden discussed it with the Soviet ambassador in London; and both governments demanded an immediate rupture of relations with the Axis countries.[62]

Third, the sheer scope of rapidly escalating Allied requirements from Iran rendered difficult, if not impossible, the retention of the shah on the throne and resulted in a significant rethinking of British policy in Iran. Up to the invasion, the British had carefully avoided raising with the Iranians their intention to use Iran's transportation network to supply the Soviet Union; they had confined themselves to pressing for the expulsion of the Germans, although the transportation network, particularly the trans-Iranian railway, was a primary objective. They saw no need of and avoided entering Tehran or involving themselves in internal administration. Once the country was partially occupied, however, and the advantages the control of Iran provided for the war effort became clear, British thinking changed dramatically. Within days of the occupation, the British chiefs of staff presented their own, extensive list of the facilities they required in Iran. These included control over or right to full use and development of all naval bases, ports, airports, railways, roads, telegraphs, and other forms of communication; the right to establish air defense systems to defend the oil fields and Abadan refinery; and the right to place Allied personnel in key communications systems.[63] Even more extensive demands were added by General Wavell, the commander-in-chief in India.[64]

Churchill, too, was already envisioning, with American help, a massive supply operation across Iran to the Soviet Union and more. On August 29, he had told Stalin that it was best if neither country entered Tehran in force, "as all we want is the through route."[65] But only six days later, he informed the War Cabinet that "Persia was now entirely in our hands, and it was clear that we must extend the scope of our original demands ... we should have complete control of Persia during the war." Unusually, he dictated a personal message to Bullard, who he thought was "not at all at the level of events" and needed "toning up."[66] He informed Bullard that the facilities required by the service chiefs had been approved and "will be drastically interpreted"; that Iran's road and rail system will be developed "at the utmost speed and at all costs" to supply Russia; that large British forces and a powerful air force would be operating out of Iran by the following year; and that the Iranian government would have to give the Allies "loyal and faithful help" to avoid an occupation of the capital. He added,

> At the present time we have not turned against the Shah but unless good results are forthcoming his mis-government of his people will be brought into the account. … our requirements must somehow be met, and it ought to be possible for you to obtain all the facilities we require, bit by bit, by using the possible leverage of a Russian occupation of Tehran.[67]

Within a few days, Eden began to lay the grounds for the Allied occupation of the capital. He informed the War Cabinet on September 8 that, given the difficulty of negotiating with the government and the unpopularity of the shah, the Allies might have to enter Tehran, "sooner or later."[68] With the Soviet ambassador in London, Ivan Maisky, he had agreed that an Allied advance into Tehran would take place on September 9, unless the Iranian government agreed to the demand that it intern German and Italian nationals and close down the four Axis legations. When the Iranians replied positively on the morning of September 9, they were given forty-eight hours to comply. Eden met with Maisky again that same morning to consider their options. If the Iranians failed to hand over the Germans and close the legations in time, Eden told Maisky, the march on Tehran could continue; or the Iranians would meet their obligations, "in which event, we should, if we wished to continue our advance to Tehran, be compelled to find some fresh reason for doing so."[69] Britain and Russia eventually agreed on a joint entry into the capital on September 16 on the grounds of Iranian noncompliance and to prevent anarchy.

At the same time, the British began to look for ways to rid themselves of Reza Shah. When Eden alerted the War Cabinet to a possible Allied entry into the capital on September 8, he also remarked that "the best solution for us would be for the Shah to take flight when our forces drew near to Tehran."[70] Discussing the same subject with Maisky on the same day, the foreign secretary told the

Soviet ambassador that if the Allies entered Tehran as planned, "it was my hope that the Shah would flee, after the style of our James II, and disembarrass us accordingly." The two governments could then "consult together about a successor."[71] The next day, Eden suggested to Maisky another solution to the Reza Shah problem: "Perhaps the best solution of all would be if the Persian politicians were to invite us into Tehran in order to carry through a coup d'état to get rid of the Shah"—a view with which Maisky agreed.[72] Following the incident over the *Ettelaat* editorial, and after Maisky observed that "the sooner the Shah went the better,"[73] Bullard was authorized to discuss a successor to Reza Shah with the Iranian government.[74] On September 15, informing the War Cabinet that British and Russian forces would enter the capital the next day, Eden added that if the shah remained in the capital, "he would be under our control" and if he tried to leave Tehran to set up an independent government elsewhere in Iran, "the Shah should be seized and held."[75]

The constitutional heir to the throne was Reza Shah's eldest son, Mohammad Reza, the crown prince; but the British now toyed with the idea of supporting someone other than the crown prince for the succession. The reasons were various and random. A chance remark by the crown prince had led Bullard erroneously to assume that Mohammad Reza Pahlavi was pro-German—an idea that registered with the Foreign Office. Some of the diplomats involved, including Maisky, had a low opinion of the crown prince's abilities. Bullard had initially attributed the damaging *Ettelaat* editorial to the crown prince. He later had to scramble to correct himself, but not before several members at the Foreign Office concluded that this rendered Mohammad Reza unsuitable for the job. "This incursion into politics on the part of the crown prince obviously rules him out as a possible successor to the Shah," Eden cabled Bullard.[76] Bullard, subjected to a cacophony of opinions among Iranians whom he was consulting, passed on to the Foreign Office the view that the shah's third son (or even one of the younger princes) was preferable to the crown prince. Finally, Leo Amery, the secretary of state for the Government of India, had got it into his head that Prince Mohammad Hassan Qajar, the younger brother of the last ruler of the Qajar dynasty that Reza Shah had overthrown in 1925, would be a better king for England than the "universally detested" Reza Shah. Bullard, Eden, and almost the entire Foreign Office staff dealing with Iran dismissed the idea as impractical and (privately) as quixotic. But in the confused British discussion of the succession, and given the doubts raised over the suitability of the crown prince, even this improbable idea enjoyed a brief moment of serious consideration. Eden finally met with Prince Hassan on September 11, cabled Bullard that "he makes a fair impression," and decided to hold him in reserve.[77] (This curious episode in Britain's attempt to unseat Reza Shah is covered in the next chapter.)

Common sense prevailed, and the day was saved for the crown prince, due to Foroughi and his foreign minister, who spoke to Bullard, and due to Bullard himself. On September 15, on the eve of the Anglo-Russian entry into Tehran, and with the expectation that Reza Shah would, as a result, abdicate, Bullard urgently cabled Eden that the crown prince would still be the best choice: "I see no better candidate for the throne at this time," he wrote.[78] The crown prince was the constitutional monarch; he would have little power, a quick succession would avoid disturbances, and his accession would be accompanied by reforms. The Soviets were on board as well. Eden agreed, two days later, that the crown prince was acceptable, but only "on trial" and on condition of "good behavior" and provided, as Bullard had suggested, there were extensive reforms, property illegally acquired by Reza Shah was restored to the nation, and Reza Shah left the country and took all his other sons with him.[79]

Reza Shah had first considered abdicating on August 26, the morning after the Anglo-Soviet invasion. He told his cabinet that he was personally the object of Anglo-Soviet hostility; and he did not want to be the cause of further misfortune for his country.[80] Yet, it is impossible to know what exactly was going through his mind. His cabinet on this occasion dissuaded him from abdicating; and perhaps he wished to be dissuaded. A month later, however, the situation had completely changed. The full extent of Allied control of Iran and their demands of the government had become clear. Reza Shah was perhaps too proud to remain king in an occupied country. Most important, he must have sensed from his prime minister (and from the BBC broadcasts) that the Allies wanted him out of the way; and that even his son's succession was at risk if he remained. Perhaps, as Bullard wrote, he feared the Russians would arrest him. On September 16, as Soviet and British forces began their move toward the capital, Reza Shah summoned his prime minister, Foroughi, to Saadabad Palace and asked him to draw up the instrument of abdication. Foroughi did so, and the shah signed it. He now impatiently paced the room, waiting for news from the telephone operator at Karaj, the last town the Russians would cross on their way to the capital. When the telephone operator called to report that Soviet troops had left Karaj, Reza Shah kissed his son and heir: "I will say goodbye."[81] He shook hands with his prime minister, entered his car, and headed for Isfahan to join his family in preparation for permanent exile.

In his memoir, *The Camels Must Go*, Sir Reader Bullard wrote that Reza Shah, on his own, elected to leave: "The common story that Riza Shah was deposed by the Allies thus seems to be baseless."[82] The weight of the evidence and Bullard's own cables suggest otherwise. True, Reza Shah, in the end, decided to abdicate; and sentiment in the country had turned against him. In his desire to maintain Iranian neutrality and Iran's links with Germany, he failed to foresee the Anglo-Soviet invasion of his country or to grasp the gravity of his situation once the Allies occupied Iran.[83] But it was Bullard who, for over many months, had made the case that association with Reza Shah was damaging to Britain's vital interests. This was a weighty consideration at a time of war. Bullard too, in language direct and indirect, repeatedly impressed on his government the desirability of getting rid of Reza Shah. Once the Allies occupied Iran, Eden looked for ways to pressure Reza Shah to leave office through flight, a British-inspired coup, or the shah's fear of the Russians. The government-directed BBC broadcasts were deliberately designed to pressure the shah and stoke popular feelings against him. Officials at the Foreign Office tossed around possible candidates for the succession: the crown prince, one of his brothers, restoration of the previous dynasty, a regency council; and they consulted with the Russians regarding a successor. Bullard, in one of his dispatches, acknowledged the key role Britain played with some local assistance. "We drove the Shah out but change was effected very capably by the Cabinet," he wrote.[84] Bullard's recommendation that the shah should cede all his wealth to the state, leave the country, and take all his other sons with him was also realized. British officials knew with near certainty that Reza Shah would abdicate if Allied troops entered the capital. On September 16, the Allies did so; and Reza Shah, as foreseen, gave up his throne.

3

"Dear Anthony," "Dear Leo": Britain's Quixotic Flirtation with Dynastic Change

As noted in the previous chapter, in weighing alternatives to Reza Shah, Britain also considered doing away with the Pahlavi dynasty altogether and restoring the Qajars to the throne. The author of this quixotic idea was Leo Amery, the secretary of state for India. In May 1941, when the British were pressing Reza Shah to expel the Germans in Iran, but before they had occupied the country, Amery penned a private note to Anthony Eden, the foreign secretary. He took as his starting point one of several cables from Bullard and the British minister's stress on Reza Shah's growing unpopularity and the serious damage that he thought Britain suffered because of its association, in the mind of Iranians, with the king. Referring disparagingly to the "universally detested" Reza Shah as Reza Khan, the shah's common name before he seized power and overthrew the ruling Qajar (Kajar) dynasty to become king in his own right, Amery wrote,

> My dear Anthony:
>
> I see from Bullard's telegram 202 that things are getting very shaky in Persia and that Reza Khan is universally detested. When considering our policy in that *connection* don't forget that the legitimate Shah, the younger brother of the late Shah, Prince Hassan Kajar, is in this country and could if necessary be flown out at any moment. He is still quite young (in the forties) and is a man who showed both courage and ability in the years in which he acted as Viceroy before being driven out … Prince Hassan might yet prove a trump card, and I know he would be willing to try his hand if we wished it.[1]

Not surprisingly, this proposal for British involvement in the restoration of a little-regretted Iranian dynasty met with a lukewarm response from Eden and his Middle East staff at the Foreign Office.[2] Yet this was not the end of the matter. Amery's quixotic proposal, initially dismissed, took on a life its own due principally to Amery's unflagging persistence but also to developments on the ground. Following the Anglo-Soviet occupation of Iran in August 1941 what began as a far-fetched idea for dynastic change was almost embraced as official British policy and came close to costing the Pahlavis the throne.

But First Some Background

The Prince Hassan to whom Amery referred was the younger brother of Ahmad Shah, the last ruler of the Qajar dynasty. Ahmad Shah had acceded to the throne in 1909 when still a minor, coming of age only in 1915. He had proved a timid and ineffective ruler who seemed to prefer the watering holes of Europe to the political machinations of Tehran. By 1921, the Qajars had been thoroughly discredited. A powerful national movement had forced Ahmad Shah's grandfather to grant the country its first constitution in 1906. Ahmad Shah's father had been deposed in 1909 after he bombarded Parliament and attempted to quash the new, hard-won constitution. Ahmad Shah himself, as already noted, had accepted a substantial monetary bribe from the British government to support the unpopular and eventually abortive Anglo-Persian Agreement of 1919, which, in the eyes of many Iranians, would have turned Iran into a British protectorate in all but name.

Two years after the 1921 coup, and with Reza Khan already virtually master of the country, Ahmad Shah had appointed Reza Khan prime minister and had departed for Europe. In his absence, his younger brother and the crown prince, Hassan, took over his duties. When in 1925 the Iranian Parliament deposed the Qajars and the monarchy was transferred to Reza Shah and the Pahlavis, Prince Hassan was unceremoniously escorted to the Iraqi border and also made his way to Europe. By 1941, he had been absent from the country for sixteen years. It was this prince, whom Amery insisted on describing as "the legitimate Shah," and this deposed dynasty that Amery proposed to bring back to power. His goal, of course, was to establish in Tehran a monarch sympathetic and pliant to Britain's war needs.

As already noted, the response at the Foreign Office to Amery's suggestion was unenthusiastic. "Prince Hassan is not a good candidate," and only heavy bribery could generate a local demand for him, noted A. V. Coverley Price, one of the Foreign Office officials in London dealing with Iran. "The mere fact that he came from England would make him persona non grata in Iran, unless he brought a shower of gold with him." His colleague, C. W. Baxter added, "I fear that the Kajar ex-Valiahd [crown prince] is by no means a strong candidate." Horace Seymour, the assistant undersecretary of state for foreign affairs, who had served as minister in Iran in 1936–9, was equally skeptical: a movement in Iran in favor of a Qajar restoration was unlikely, he noted. Moreover, British promotion of dynastic change in Iran could lead to Russian intervention.[3] Eden took his time—two weeks—to reply to Amery. His note, incorporating the views of his staff, particularly Seymour's, was polite but dismissive:

> My dear Leo:
>
> The Qajar candidate might possibly be useful in the event of any movement in Persia for the return of the Qajar dynasty. I think, however, that such a movement is unlikely. It seems more probable that, when the Shah loses his grip, the Pahlevi dynasty will be succeeded by some general who is able to seize power. This is the normal thing in Persian history.
>
> I would not be in favor of an attempt by us to promote a revolution in Persia, especially as this would very likely result in Russian intervention.[4]

Amery, however, was not to be deterred; and this resulted in an exchange over several months of personal notes between "dear Anthony" and "dear Leo." Amery continued to press his case for a Qajar restoration under Prince Hassan (or possibly under his younger son, Prince Hamid), and Eden and his Middle East staff at the Foreign Office continued politely to discourage what they regarded as an impractical idea. In pursuit of his cause, Amery in time tried to enlist the support of British diplomats, retired and active, who had served in Iran; he invoked an endorsement for his cause from the Government of India; and he even pressed the idea on Prime Minister Churchill—all to little effect. Yet this was hardly the end of the matter. Events played into Amery's hands; and what initially seemed improbable and impractical became, for a moment, a possibility, then almost a reality.

Operation Barbarossa, as noted, turned Russia and Britain into allies. Both countries were disturbed by the large German presence in Iran and now joined hands to pressure Reza Shah to send the Germans home. The allies also wished to employ the Iranian road network and particularly the recently completed trans-Iranian railway to supply an embattled Russia with arms and other essential requirements. Unable to secure Reza Shah's cooperation regarding the Germans and urgently in need of a supply route to the Soviet Union, Britain and the USSR began to coordinate pressure on the shah and, already by the last week of July, to plan for the use of military force if necessary. This provided Amery with an opening to revive the idea of a Qajar restoration.

On July 25, he noted in his diary, "Spoke again to Anthony about Prince Hassan: he has obviously done nothing and is not very alive to possibilities there."[5] In another note to "dear Anthony" on July 30, after weighing in on the advisability of military action, Amery once again proposed setting up Prince Hassan as king. "Please don't forget that we have a possible Pretender here in the legitimate Shah, Prince Hassan, if the present Shah should prove really recalcitrant … [Prince Hassan] could of course be flown out very quickly." Amery wasn't quite sure where Hassan lived, but he offered, discreetly, to find his address, "as we know him quite well personally."[6] He followed this letter up with a handwritten note to Eden, suggesting the Foreign Office consult British diplomats who had served in Iran and who knew Prince Hassan when he was crown prince: "I think the best way of finding out how far he is likely to be acceptable in Persia, if we have to hash with Reza [Shah], is to ask Havard … or Percy Loraine. All I can say is that he is a very nice fellow, intelligent and undoubtedly our way."[7]

The Foreign Office remained unconvinced. Seymour pointed out that consulting Percy Loraine, a former minister to Tehran, or Godfrey Havard, who had served as oriental secretary at the Tehran legation and was now consul general in Beirut, would be pointless, since Loraine had left Iran in 1926 and Havard in 1933. Seymour thought the opinion of the diplomats in Tehran would more relevant than that of people "who have no present acquaintance with a rapidly changing situation."[8] Bullard, the British minister in Tehran, was in due course consulted. His response was unhelpful to Amery's cause: "There is no enthusiasm for the Qajar [dynasty] … and it is doubtful that any member of the family would find much local support," he cabled to London.[9] Seymour seconded Bullard's assessment: "It does not look as if we should do much good by sending anyone of this family to Persia as our candidate," he wrote. If Reza

Shah went, he noted, succession by his eldest son, Mohammad Reza, would avoid confusion and suit England for that reason.[10]

Amery, however, persisted. Bullard's views may be useful on Qajar prospects in general, he wrote to Eden, but it was Loraine and particularly Havard who could speak to "Prince Hassan's personality and power of handling his own people which of course Bullard couldn't." Again, he urged Havard be consulted.[11] The Foreign Office demurred. There was no point in consulting Havard, C. W. Baxter noted, "since, whatever reply we received, the fact remains that Prince Hassan's chances of mounting the throne are practically nil."[12] Amery also seems to have tried to enlist the support of Harold Nicolson, the retired diplomat and distinguished author, who had served as counsellor in the Tehran legation in 1925–7 and was currently a member of Parliament and a governor of the BBC. It was perhaps at Amery's instigation that Prince Hassan called on Nicolson in early August to say that should Britain "adopt an attitude of hostility to Reza Shah and the Pahlevi dynasty … there is an alternative Shah, waiting for us and anxious to help." Nicolson, writing of this visit in a "dear Anthony" note to Eden, also referred to Hassan as "the legitimate King of Kings"; but Nicolson was more cautious than Amery in advocating Hassan's candidacy. The prince, he noted, made no concrete proposals and was a bit vague. Moreover, Nicolson observed, while Reza Shah's crown prince, Mohammad Reza, was married to the king of Egypt's sister, Prince Hassan's second son and the putative heir of the Qajar dynasty (Hamid) was a British subject and had served in a branch of British merchant navy, under the name of Mr. Drummond. "How it came about that the King of Kings was so careless about his dynastic progeny as to allow his Valiahd [crown prince] to become a member of the British Merchant Navy and to speak no language except English, passes my comprehension."[13]

Eden, replying in similar letters to both "My dear Leo" and "My dear Harold" on August 18, reiterated Bullard's view that there would be little support among Iranians for a Qajar prince and that the current crown prince would be the best candidate should Reza Shah vacate the throne. "This is also my personal view," Eden added in his note to Amery. "I can recall no example in Persian history of a 'hark back' to an earlier dynasty." To Nicolson, he said, regarding Prince Hassan, "I don't like the idea of saddling ourselves with a candidate who might collapse at the first opposition," although "we should keep our hands free till we see how things are likely to shape."[14]

A disappointed Amery noted in his diary, "The FO at present favoring [Reza Shah's] son ... and refusing to consider my friend Prince Hassan";[15] however, he would not let the matter drop. Failing to secure from Reza Shah the expulsion of the Germans and in need of Iran's through routes, Britain and Russia invaded Iran on August 25 and occupied the country, although they initially refrained from entering the capital. That same morning, or the next day, Amery followed up with a telephone call to the Foreign Office and, unable to speak to Eden, spoke instead to Seymour. Adding a new twist to his advocacy, Amery was now also promoting Prince Hassan's younger son, Hamid, as a candidate for the throne, possibly as an early successor to his father.[16] Hamid was the young man who, as Nicolson had noted, was raised in England, spoke no Persian, and had served in the British merchant navy under the name of David Drummond.

Seymour reported on this telephone conversation with Amery in a note to Eden's private secretary, Oliver Harvey. Amery, he wrote, had met Hamid and was urging that Eden or someone else at the Foreign Office meet with him as well. "Mr. Amery had been very much impressed with the young man who was he thought an excellent type and extremely English in outlook and appearance." Seymour added, "I do not quite see what I am to say to this young man if I see him, nor do I think a typically English outlook and appearance is at all a good asset for a claimant to the throne of the King of Kings."[17] Eden's reaction to Amery new overture was at once bemused and impatient; yet, as usual, he wished to keep his options open. On Seymour's memo, he penned a note to his staff: "I found L. Amery pouring all this stuff into P. M.'s ear when I arrived at [the prime minister's residence at] No. 10 Downing. I rebuked him! But we may as well have this young man in mind but not see him until we decide that we want to unseat the Shah."[18]

Amery's push for dynastic change in Iran did receive support from one major participant in these exchanges, the Government of India. Both before and after the Anglo-Soviet occupation of Iran, India had argued for a policy toward Iran more forceful than the gradualist and nuanced approach favored by the Foreign Office. An impatient India government at one stage even accused the Foreign Office of "appeasement" toward the Iranian government. India, for example, argued early for using economic pressure to secure the expulsion of the Germans—a policy the Foreign Office concluded would not be effective, at least not quickly enough and if not backed up by the threat of force. India was also an early proponent for demanding from the Iranians the use of the Iranian road network and the trans-Iranian railway to supply the USSR, a demand Eden thought it wiser to raise only after the German issue had been addressed. When the invasion took place, the Government of India joined the chiefs of staff in calling for extensive demands on the Iranian government including the control of communications lines, ports, and airports and occupation of large parts of the country.[19]

The Government of India was much impressed by Bullard's frequent assertions that Britain suffered standing and sympathy among Iranians because of its association with Reza Shah. Against this background, it embraced Amery's idea of unseating Reza Shah and the Pahlavi dynasty and restoring the Qajars.

In late August, following the Anglo-Soviet occupation of Iran, Amery was pleased to send to Eden a copy of a cable from the viceroy in India, Lord Linlithgow, who, "not on any instigation of mine," Amery wrote, endorsed the Hassan candidacy. Linlithgow in fact echoed Amery's views and, as Eden was later to remark, showed little appreciation of the realities on the ground in Iran. Linlithgow wrote,

> Question whether we should continue to deal with the Shah is issue of fundamental importance. ... We suggest question of restoration of Qajar dynasty might have possibilities ... Mohammad Hassan was Prince Regent in Tehran [prior to] accession of Reza Shah and though absent from Persia for some 16 years had some reputation for dignity and statesmanship. Restoration of the old regime might succeed in some degree in rallying natives and hereditary leaders of the country.[20]

In a "dear Anthony" cover letter enclosing the Linlithgow cable, Amery added further words of support for Prince Hassan's claim and the Qajars in general: "Remember they are not merely a family, but a large tribe, numbering I believe hundreds of thousands ... presumably they would support a restoration." As to Prince Hassan, "I know him as a charming, courteous gentleman ... and generally pretty shrewd. As to his sons, they are quite remarkable specimens of fine, virile Englishmen (in all except complexion)."[21]

At the Foreign Office, H. A. Caccia, Eden's assistant private secretary, noted that Reza Shah had destroyed the power of the tribes, rendering them unimportant, and wryly added, "The fact that the young Qajars are 'fine, virile young Englishmen' surely puts them out of the running for the Persian throne? It would make them thoroughly suspect to the Russians as well as to the Persians." In a handwritten note in the red ink he often used, Eden also was dismissive of India's views, although he did not entirely close the door on the Qajar option. "The pressure grows," he wrote. "Tho[ugh] India is notoriously wrong on all matters Persian, we may consider it desirable to give this further thought. We may not be able to buttress the Shah, and then what?"[22]

To recap, then: up to and even after the Anglo-Soviet occupation of Iran Amery's advocacy for a Qajar restoration had met with a decidedly cool reception at the Foreign Office and at the legation in Tehran. Both thought there was little support in Iran for Prince Hassan or for a return of the Qajars. Hassan personally aroused little enthusiasm; and while Amery thought it an asset that Hassan's sons were "two hefty, vigorous boys … thoroughly English in their outlook,"[23] Eden's staff considered the "Englishness" of Hassan's sons a decided disadvantage for claimants to the Iranian throne.

Eden it is true, as was his wont, left his options open; but he offered no encouragement to Amery in his several "dear Leo" notes, nor to Nicolson. His minutes, addressed to his own staff, suggest exasperation with Amery's importunities and his attempt to win Churchill over to his cause. Eden's remark that the Government of India tended to be "notoriously wrong on all things Persian" was not misplaced. Both India and Amery seemed to imagine an Iran of decades earlier. India, for example, looked improbably to "natives and hereditary leaders" to rally to the Qajars, and Amery seemed under the illusion that the Qajars were still a large tribe of tens of thousands, when in reality the Qajars no longer functioned as a tribe. Numerous members of the former royal family remained; but Qajar tribal solidarity had long dissipated. Yet, on September 11, two weeks into the Anglo-Soviet occupation of Iran, Eden agreed to meet with Prince Hassan and his son Hamid over lunch at Amery's house and, afterward, to entertain the possibility of putting the Qajars back on the throne. He cabled Bullard,

> Prince Hassan Qajar, the heir of the Qajar dynasty is in London and I have met with him and his son privately. He makes a fair impression. The son is an excellent type, but is Europeanized and does not speak Persian.
>
> Prince Hassan would be prepared to go to Persia if there was a movement for replacing the Qajar dynasty on the throne. He would take his son with

him … I do not (repeat not) wish you to discuss this possibility either with Persians or with your Soviet colleague at present but I should like your own views as to possibilities.[24]

Prince Hamid's recollections of this meeting, recorded in a lengthy interview he gave some four decades later, are understandably fuzzy on some of the details, but remain nevertheless instructive. They confirm that the discussion that day touched on the possible return of Hassan to Iran and his installation as shah; and they also help us understand why Eden was eager to learn from Hassan whether, if he was returned to Iran, he would take Hamid back with him. There had been several meetings between his father and various British officials, Hamid recalled, and added,

> One day, after lunch in London with Sir Anthony Eden and various other members of the British cabinet, my father and I, walking through Green Park, honestly thought that the next day we would be asked to return to Tehran …
>
> I think the intention was to take back my father, but with a limited stay, as he was too colored by the older elements of the dynasty. And to try that approach first … before putting in a younger man of the newer generation … the impression I got was [that] it would be me.[25]

Hamid and his father clearly read more than warranted into this meeting. Eden at this point had not yet made up his mind; he was still exploring his options. But the possibility of a Qajar restoration was now on the table, as was the idea that Hamid might replace his father on the throne after an interval. That evening, Amery noted in his diary that "the lunch went off very well, Anthony evidently liked young Hamid and had a really good talk afterwards with his father … Bullard is now being sounded as to the possibility of a Qajar restoration being spontaneously mooted from the Persian side."[26] Eden's deputy private secretary, Caccia, noted on September 13, "Yesterday Sir R. Bullard was given authority to discuss question of succession—'including possibility of Prince Hassan.'"[27]

This dramatic turnaround at the Foreign Office—from the initial dismissal of Amery's proposal as far-fetched and impractical to its near embrace—requires explanation. Bullard had continued to hammer home his view of Reza Shah's unpopularity; the harm association with him did to Britain's standing with the Iranian people; and the desirability of unseating him. Once the Anglo-Soviet occupation of Iran took place, Bullard also concluded that Reza Shah was obstructing Allied objectives in Iran, confirming his belief that Reza Shah must go. By the first week of September, he had won over the Foreign Office to his view, and Eden began to look for ways to bring about Reza Shah's flight or abdication. The Allies in fact secured Reza Shah's abdication when they finally sent their troops to occupy the capital on September 16—a step they had until then avoided. It was in this context—in the anticipation of and planning for the post-Reza Shah period—that Eden met with Prince Hassan and his son, Hamid, and cabled Bullard for his views regarding a Qajar restoration.

The crown prince, Mohammad Reza, was the constitutional successor to the throne. However, Bullard had inadvertently created the impression at the Foreign Office that the crown prince would for various reasons be unsuitable for the succession. He reported to London the Russian ambassador's unfavorable impression of the crown prince's abilities. He erroneously attributed to Mohammad Reza Pahlavi pro-German sympathies and a role in obstructing Allied objectives in Iran.[28] On all these points, Bullard later scrambled to correct himself, but not before the damage was done. When the Anglo-Soviet entry into Tehran precipitated Reza Shah's hasty abdication, Eden cabled Bullard that the crown prince was unacceptable as shah and asked for, and himself proposed, alternatives:

> As regards succession, it seems to us that the Crown Prince must be ruled out on account of his well-known pro-German sympathies and we cannot regard Shah's abdication in favor of his son as anything but a ruse to prolong anti-Allied policy … As we see it, possible alternative would be one of the younger Pahlevis or a Qajar restoration. Prince Hassan strikes me as tractable and intelligent but not as a strong personality, while his son Hamid is an excellent type, but speaks no Persian.[29]

Ironically, it was Bullard, instrumental in persuading the Foreign Office to force Reza Shah from the throne, who now helped preserve the crown for the Pahlavis. Bullard thought highly of the man the shah had appointed as prime minister immediately following the Anglo-Soviet invasion. Mohammad Ali Foroughi was a respected elder statesman and scholar; and Bullard felt that both Foroughi and his foreign minister, Ali Soheili, were sincere in their desire to cooperate with the Allies and to begin a program of reform. The two men had shared with Bullard, in language both direct and indirect, their impatience with Reza Shah, their conviction that the shah remained an obstacle to change, and their wish to see him go. Soheili had told Bullard that, in the right circumstances, Reza Shah could be persuaded to abdicate.[30] Foroughi himself seems to have concluded that the intensity of British hostility to Reza Shah made it impossible for him to remain on the throne.[31] Judging by Bullard's dispatches, these two men appear to have played a key role in convincing Bullard that the sensible policy would be to allow the succession of Mohammad Reza to go forward unimpeded.

Bullard laid out the arguments for acquiescing in the crown prince's succession in a quick cable to the Foreign Office on September 15, when he thought Reza Shah's abdication imminent and a decision by Britain on the succession urgent.[32] He followed up with a lengthier, more detailed cable two days later.[33] His first cable proved sufficient to persuade Eden to reverse his decision (Bullard's second cable crossed the one from Eden to him), but the full case made by Bullard is worth reviewing. It provides some insight into the influence of Foroughi (and Soheili) on Bullard's thinking; and it helps show why Amery's "Qajar project" was from the beginning misconceived. Bullard argued that succession by the crown prince would have the benefit of legitimacy, conforming to the course of action laid down in the constitution. It would be the least disturbing to a country already disrupted by the Allied invasion. By insisting on another choice, Britain would make itself responsible for the new ruler's actions and involve itself in "a mass of conflicting interests and intrigues." There was no demand for a Qajar ruler; the prime minister opposed a return of the dynasty; and even though the British could force the country to accept a Qajar (Bullard, here, seems to have been referring to Prince Hamid), "I should have thought his ignorance of Persia a serious bar and his English education a source of embarrassment sooner or later both with the Persians and Russians." Besides, there were "hundreds of Qajars in the country … waiting hungrily … for return of the days when the country was bled not by one leech but by hundreds." The crown prince would be a constitutional monarch with few powers and would prove tractable due to his youth and inexperience and the lesson he learned from the fate of his father; and Prime Minister Foroughi thought well of his abilities, goodwill, and readiness to begin reforms. There was, also, Bullard noted, the danger that, despite their protestations to the contrary, the Soviets would have preferred violent change. Locking in the succession would avoid that possibility.

Bullard's arguments proved persuasive. Eden cabled Bullard on September 17 that "in view of the difficulty of finding any other solution," the crown prince was acceptable, but only on trial and "subject to good behavior," and on condition he instituted reforms and remained a constitutional monarch with little power.[34]

That Eden and the Foreign Office were so quick to reverse themselves on the acceptability of the crown prince is not difficult to explain. In addition to the arguments advanced by Bullard, Hassan had made a passable but not a strong impression during lunch with Eden and his aides; Hamid's lack of familiarity with Iran or the Persian language was a serious obstacle to a Qajar restoration.[35] The Iranians themselves effectively preempted the British by quickly swearing in Mohammad Reza as shah on September 17, the day after Reza Shah's abdication. Although Bullard, in urging London to give the new king a chance, wrote that "we could always get rid of him quickly if he proved unsuitable,"[36] such a move obviously became more difficult once the crown prince took his oath of office before Parliament and was seated on the throne.

Besides, a perusal of the record suggests that in the weeks immediately preceding and following the Anglo-Soviet occupation of Iran, considerable uncertainty prevailed at the Foreign Office as to what set of circumstances might cause Reza Shah's departure or what might ensue if he abdicated or was forced from the throne. Bullard and his influential press attaché, Ann Lambton, did not rule out a popular movement to oust the shah (which never materialized). Some thought the shah might be murdered (another highly unlikely scenario). Coverley Price foresaw chaos on the shah's departure and the emergence of a German puppet. Seymour believed some general might seize control (though no such attempt occurred) or that the British might need to back up "some local leader who seems to have a following and a chance." I. T. M. Pink, another Foreign Office official dealing with Iran, thought that if Reza Shah went, "it was essential to make a clean sweep of the whole 'Pahlevi' brood." Eden and others thought Reza Shah might be succeeded by a British-backed regency under a prominent Iranian statesman.[37]

While too much need not be made of such bewildering speculation, it reflects the uncertainty prevailing at the Foreign Office regarding the best course of action should Reza Shah go. This left men at the Foreign Office open to suggestions and persuasion—from Amery, from Bullard, from others— regarding the post-Reza Shah period. This can help explain why, despite much initial skepticism, Eden finally gave serious consideration to, then quickly abandoned, Amery's campaign for a Qajar restoration—and why, in the end, the decisive argument for retaining the Pahlavis on the throne was made not in London but in Tehran.

4

The Journey into Exile

Reza Shah's journey into exile took him from Tehran to Isfahan, where he spent four nights, and thence to Yazd (two nights) and Kerman in eastern Iran (three nights). From Kerman, Reza Shah expected to cross overland through Baluchistan into India, where he intended to spend some two weeks "sightseeing" before taking a ship into permanent exile in South America. In Isfahan, Yazd, and Kerman, the royal party was housed in the homes of prominent merchants or local dignitaries. But this was hardly a glittering royal progress. The departure of the women and children from Tehran was hurried; members of the royal family took very little baggage with them. About to leave the country, they didn't even have passports. (Both baggage and passports followed later.) Preparations for the royal family as they journeyed south were helter-skelter. The governor of Kerman was told to prepare to house the shah, but he was not told how many were in the royal party or how long they would stay; and while two prominent merchants in Kerman, contacted by the governor, offered to host Reza Shah, several others refused to do so.[1] In the hurry to leave, Princess Fawzia, the crown prince's Egyptian wife, left behind on the grounds of the royal palace a box of her personal jewelry, where a court official later came across it. Fereydoun Jam, the shah's son-in-law and the only adult male family member accompanying the women and children, had to cadge scarce gasoline from friends along the way.[2] After a tiring fourteen-hour journey, the royal party arrived in Isfahan at midnight, spent another hour before they cleared security checkpoints, and, having nowhere else to go, spent the remaining part of the night at the military base, before a leading merchant of the Kazerouni family put his house at their disposal.[3]

Reza Shah, following six days later, rode alone with his driver, without the usual escort. On the road to Qum, his tires twice developed punctures and eventually broke down, requiring king and driver to commandeer another car.

A lunch of eggs and bread on a tin tray had to be purchased for the king of kings from a roadside teahouse.[4] His son-in-law, Jam, who went to greet him some 50–60 kilometers outside of Isfahan, encountered the shah, alone, descending from a battered old car, carrying a briefcase and a military "swagger stick." Jam writes that when he saw Reza Shah—for him, the epitome of power and majesty—reduced to such a condition, he was driven to tears.[5] In Kerman, the military commander, uncertain whether and in what manner he should greet the ex-shah, found reason to leave the city.[6]

Having abdicated, Reza Shah was under the impression that he was free to elect his own place of exile. The young women of the family had settled on Chile or Argentina—countries they thought suitable due to climate and that lay outside the war zone, but with which the royal family had but the vaguest acquaintance; and visas for Argentina were being issued even as the royal family made their way into exile.[7] Reza Shah seemed to be thinking of taking up agriculture once settled in South America. "Fereydoun," he said to his son-in-law who was a military officer, "when we go to Argentine or Chile, you must take up farming. Soldiering is over for you."[8]

The British, however, had no intention of allowing Reza Shah to go to South America or any neutral country where he might become the center of intrigue and the target of "Nazi agents and propagandists, political intriguers and journalists."[9] They wanted him to remain firmly in British hands; and this argued for exile somewhere in the British Empire. India was initially considered; but the viceroy, Lord Linlithgow, refused to allow the exiled shah to set foot on Indian soil. "He would be simply a gift for Jinnah and those Moslems who want to make trouble for us over Persia," wrote Leo Amery, the secretary of state for India, reflecting the viceroy's views.[10]

Lord Linlithgow did not even want Reza Shah anywhere near the Indian border. In a telegram to the secretary of state for India he described Reza Shah's planned travel to the Indian frontier as a "thoroughly ill-considered project in present circumstances. Ex-Shah arrival in Baluchistan would cause us grave embarrassment … we should prefer not to have him in this country at all." The ex-shah, he thought, should be sent elsewhere—anywhere but India. He recommended that Reza Shah be redirected to the Iranian port city of Bushehr and the sea route. "This would give us time to consider whether ship might be diverted elsewhere (e.g. Ceylon) in order to accelerate his journey onward."[11]

He followed up with a telegram the following day: "Government of India regard it as of extreme importance that the Shah be diverted to the sea route."[12]

The Foreign Office (FO) pleaded for India to allow Reza Shah to enter the country briefly while they tried to arrange for another place of exile: "Every effort will be made to relieve you of this liability without delay," the FO wrote.[13] But the viceroy was adamant: "We are still strongly opposed to the ex-Shah living in India even temporarily," he cabled back.[14] The Government of India had already located a ship, the SS *Bandra*, and, rather than to Bushehr, had diverted it to Bandar Abbas, the Iranian port nearest to Kerman, to pick up the shah and his party. While recognizing that the *Bandra* would need to refuel at Bombay port en route to wherever Reza Shah would be taken, the viceroy also emphasized that the vessel must refuel well offshore: "Ex-Shah will not be allowed to land," he wrote.[15]

At the FO, India's refusal to accommodate Reza Shah set off a scramble to find him another place of exile. The FO and the Colonial Office (CO) sent off cables to British officials in Kenya, Northern Rhodesia, Mauritius, and even Seychelles. Kenya begged off due to the presence in the colony of large Arab, Indian, and Somali Muslim communities. Rhodesia lacked the necessary accommodations for such a large party; moreover, the route was difficult. Seychelles was ruled out due to climate and primitive conditions.[16] The governor of Mauritius, Sir Bede Clifford, came to the rescue. He offered to accommodate the ex-shah, and Clifford's superiors at the CO agreed.

The resources available in Mauritius were, however, meager. Clifford asked that the royal party bring with them

> pillows, bed linen, blankets, bath and face towels, napkins, table cloths, dust and kitchen cloths, 150 feet of stair carpet, rugs, mattresses. Size of mattresses should be telegraphed in advance as beds to suit will have to be made locally.[17]

In Kerman, Reza Shah was not informed that he would not be allowed into India. He was told only that the overland route was inconvenient and that he was being diverted to the sea route. He acquiesced in this decision without protest. By now the fierce and formidable ruler, whose temper used to leave his ministers quaking with fear, had grown decidedly less imperious. Something inside "the lion of Persia" had broken. His country had been invaded and occupied. His beloved army had collapsed. Under Allied pressure and perhaps to preserve the throne for his son,[18] he had abdicated and, no longer in control, was now leaving his country. Long in command and used to giving the orders, he now seemed resigned to have others take decisions for him.

A Suddenly Aged Man

His eldest daughters Shams and Ashraf saw before them a stooped, suddenly aged man.[19] He no longer was given to his fits of ferocious anger. For the first time in the memory of those around him he complained that he was tired. For the first time, family members and others saw tears in his eyes. He walked a great deal in the gardens and paced along the hallways of the homes where he stayed and seemed frequently deep in thought.[20] He grew dismissive of the trappings of royalty that had surrounded him. "Bring it down," he later said, seeing his picture on the wall in the office of the director of customs at Bandar Abbas. "There is no need of my picture anymore." He waved away the honor guard present at his final departure: "What is all this for? It's not at all necessary."[21] He told a senior government officer who came to see him on official business but feared incurring his displeasure, "Don't be afraid. I don't count for anything anymore."[22] The minister of roads, Mohammad Sajjadi, who needed his signature on property transfer papers, and who as a cabinet minister had often been received in audience on official business or to be given instructions, was surprised that the old formality was gone. "On that day," he recalled, "Reza Shah spoke to me as a friend."[23]

In Isfahan, emissaries from his son, the new shah, arrived by prearrangement for Reza Shah to sign the necessary documents transferring to his successor all his enormous personal wealth—bank accounts, landholdings, agricultural enterprises, factories—to be used for the welfare of the people. He did so without a murmur, but it clearly bothered him to be rendered, in effect, penniless and dependent on the generosity of his son. "I worked hard; I amassed wealth," he told Abol-Qasem Harandi, his host in Kerman, "and now that I want to go abroad, I have no money." To the promptings of the British consul in Kerman, George Falconer, who was trying to hurry him on his way out of the country, he responded angrily, "Where am I to go? I haven't five rials in my pocket."[24]

Hungry for news, he listened regularly to broadcasts from Radio Tehran and the BBC Persian service or had his son-in-law listen and report to him. The BBC continued its barrage of unfavorable commentary on Reza Shah's misdeeds as ruler. "What is this hue and cry? What does this British radio want of me?" he asked.[25] According to the minister of court, Mahmoud Jam (Fereydoun's father), the ex-shah was "made unhappy beyond description" by reports, deliberately encouraged by the BBC, that the royal family was leaving Iran with suitcases of valuable items from the Crown Jewels. This collection constituted a priceless assemblage of diamonds, rubies, emeralds, and other precious stones, including the Darya-e-Nur, one of the world's largest uncut diamonds; bejeweled necklaces, pins, tiaras, and royal crowns; and gem-studded objects such as vases, goblets, jewel boxes, and a globe of the world in gold and encrusted with over fifty thousand gemstones. Deputies in the Majlis, or the Parliament, picked up on these reports and insisted the "missing" jewels be returned. But the reports were untrue. When the Allies invaded, Reza Shah had arranged for the transfer of the Crown Jewels from the royal museum to the vaults of the national bank for safe keeping. A meticulous inventory had been taken in the presence of cabinet ministers and court and museum officials and checked against existing lists. Reza Shah now instructed the prime minister to conduct a second inventory in the presence of Majlis deputies. Nothing was found missing.[26] On Tehran radio, the shah heard Majlis deputies, who only recently had been fawning on him, calling for him to be put on trial. He was upset by the remarks of two deputies whom he had instructed be "elected" to the Parliament for two successive terms: "Did you hear what they are saying behind my back?" he asked his host in Kerman.[27]

Otherwise, Reza Shah stuck to his usual strict schedule: he went to bed at 10 p.m. and rose at 5 or 6 in the morning. He had his usual breakfast of a glass of tea and toast and he lunched, alone, on rice and stews. He always walked in the garden in the morning, and often at other times as well, though family members made sure he was not alone. As always, he slept not in a bed, but on the floor, on a small rug that always traveled with him.[28] He continued to worry that the projects he had begun would not be completed; he sent brief messages to his son, the new king, about things that needed attention in the places where he stayed on his journey out of the country—weak electric power in one town, dilapidated wharves in a port city. With his hosts, officials, and members of his family, he reminisced about his early years as a soldier, his hopes for the country, and what he had done for it. He seemed exercised to address well-founded criticism that he had amassed wealth and vast properties in northern Iran by questionable methods and that his rule had been harsh and autocratic.

He had been a simple soldier, he told the minister, Sajjadi, "who fought for the survival of the country alongside hundreds of other shoeless and hungry soldiers, on mule, and behind machine-gun and cannon." He had risen out of the poor and lower classes himself. "How was it possible that I should not care for the people and not be at war throughout my reign with the demons of unemployment and ignorance?"[29] Listening on Tehran radio to the attacks on him by newly emboldened Majlis deputies, he remarked bitterly, "I no sooner set foot outside Tehran than the same persons who always and everywhere praised me and were sycophantic about my work and actions are now singing a different song."[30] He told the prominent carpet merchant in Kerman who had provided the rugs for the house in which he was staying that he had revived Iran's carpet industry and rescued it from destruction by foreign competition. The national bank he had established, he said, revived the Iranian economy. In his lengthy conversation with Sajjadi while in Isfahan, he conceded he had acquired and cultivated vast properties in northern Iran—but as a shield against Russian influence, he said, and to show people it was possible to work hard and be productive.[31] When he asked of "bad" things he might have done during his reign, Sajjadi mentioned that peasants on his properties had been "brought to their knees" by the cruel exploitation they suffered at the hands of overseers. "You are right. You are right," Reza Shah replied, and execrated his overseers for assuring him that his peasants were all "praying for me" even when reports reached him of the mistreatment of peasants on his lands.[32] He thought he had nurtured good relations with Iran's two powerful neighbors, Russia and Britain, he told his host in Kerman: "Now do you see what our neighbors have done to us?"[33] he asked.

At times he fell back on caustic humor, often directed at himself. In Kerman, it so happened that the notary public, a photographer, and an army physician who were summoned to the house where he was staying, each walked with a limp. "All our affairs are limping," Reza Shah remarked.[34] He could even indirectly acknowledge his well-known penchant for expropriating property or land that he coveted or forcing owners to sell to him at ruinously low prices. "Had I known you have such a fine house," he told his host in Isfahan, "I would have told them to take it from you."[35]

By the time Reza Shah and his family gathered in Kerman and set off for Bandar Abbas, the royal party was large. There was the shah, his wife, her half sister and a lady-in-waiting; six sons and three daughters, ranging from 24 to 10 years in age; his son-in-law, Jam, and his private secretary, Izadi; a cook, half a dozen servants; and several cars and two truckloads of baggage and household goods.[36] (Princess Fawzia had returned to Tehran to rejoin her husband, the new shah.) Mishaps, discomforts, and humiliations continued. In Yazd, Reza Shah developed an earache and a fever, which persisted until he left Iran. The journey from Kerman to Bandar Abbas stretched across 550 kilometers of dirt road, requiring a sleepover at the small town of Sirjan; and the heat everywhere was intense. On the road to Sirjan, the truck carrying food supplies and gear overturned; a cook ended up with a broken arm, a couple of other servants were injured, and the ex-shah's special rice spilled down a ravine.[37] According to Princess Shams, lunches along the road were eaten at "poor" teahouses and at an equally unappealing gendarmerie post.[38] Leaving Kerman well after the rest of the royal party, the court minister, Mahmoud Jam, arrived in Sirjan too late to join them at the home where they were housed and had to sleep on the floor in the telegraph office.[39]

As he made his way to Bandar Abbas, Reza Shah also had to put up with humiliating pestering from the young British consul, Falconer, who, instructed by India, was impatient to see Reza Shah out of the country. "What's the hurry?" Reza Shah reacted angrily. "I am going. Did I say I would not go?"[40] Falconer even warned that the SS *Bandra* would sail without the ex-shah if he did not arrive at Bandar Abbas and board by September 26—"an unauthorized threat which I think was justified in the circumstances," Falconer later explained to his ambassador.[41] Due to the unfounded reports that the royal family was leaving the country with national treasures, and on instructions from Tehran, customs officers at Bandar Abbas examined the family's baggage, trunk-by-trunk and suitcase-by-suitcase, itemizing everything from beds and bedding, pots and pans, china and cutlery to personal jewelry, clothing, toiletries, and listing even a water flask and a shaving kit.[42]

The ex-shah and his party arrived at Bandar Abbas at night on September 26, and the women and children boarded ship just after midnight. Reza Shah wished to spend his last night in Iran on Iranian soil and did not board until 7 a.m. the next morning. For the first time in the memory of members of his family, he discarded his military uniform and appeared in civilian clothes, wearing one of the suits, "all ill-fitting," that a tailor had sewn for him in Isfahan.[43] Because the wharf was too shallow to accommodate the *Bandra*, the passengers had to get to the ship by motor launch; and the three automobiles that the shah and his sons wanted to take with them—one of them a Cadillac, another a Mercedes Benz—had to be laboriously loaded at high tide on barges and then transferred to the ship. Bandar Abbas was experiencing unusual heat and humidity. Falconer worried about the shah's "unfortunate" minister of court, who was dressed, he wrote, "in a suit more suitable for winter in Tehran than summer in Bandar Abbas," and whom he found pleasant "but inclined to drink a little too much." He persuaded Mahmoud Jam "to try tea for his breakfast on board instead of whiskey and soda."[44]

The small 5,000-ton *Bandra*, of the British India Steam Navigation Company, was primarily a cargo ship that during the war was being used for the transport of personnel as well. On this voyage, the royal party had it to themselves. The captain and most of the officers were English; the crew was Indian. Princess Shams described it as "a poor, wretched vessel"[45] but the five-day trip passed without incident. The family ate in the small dining room and retired at night to their cabins. Reza Shah, as always, ate alone in his own small room, spent much of the day pacing back and forth on the deck, and preferred to sleep under the open sky, his bedding spread on the floor of the deck. On the morning of October 2, Shams and others caught sight of Bombay in the distance.

Clarmont Skrine's Mission

At Bombay port, the *Bandra* was required to anchor 6 miles offshore. Naval guards boarded the ship; a patrol boat circled the *Bandra*; and the ship's own boats were lowered to prevent anyone from leaving. The British were exercised to keep secret Reza Shah's presence and the decision to send him to Mauritius. No one, not even the captain, was allowed to disembark. A larger ship, the SS *Burma*, was expected in a few days to carry the family on the longer voyage to Mauritius.

The governor of Mauritius, Bede Clifford, had asked that a Persian-speaking British official accompany Reza Shah to the island. This assignment fell to Clarmont Skrine, a veteran of the Indian political service, who had served in Iran in the 1920s as vice-consul in Kerman and consul in Sistan. He knew Persian, but he hadn't used it in over a decade. His Persian was rusty; he spoke it with a heavy accent, and it turned out Reza Shah could not easily understand him.

It fell to Skrine to break the news to Reza Shah that he would not be allowed to enter India and was going to Mauritius instead. A stormy interview ensued. Skrine reported that when the family

> at last realized what was to be their fate and had found Mauritius in their atlas there was a most unpleasant scene in which the whole family, down to the ten-year old Hamid Reza took part, abusing the British in general and me in particular for what the Shah described as typical English perfidy.

Reza Shah protested that he had abdicated on the understanding that he would be allowed to proceed to South America; he asserted he would never have agreed to leave Iran had he known he was to be made "a prisoner of war" and sent off to "an island of which he had never heard."[46] He sent a telegram of protest to the viceroy and a second telegram to his son, asking him to intervene.[47] Skrine's assurances that there was no intention of treating the royal family as political prisoners, and that Mauritius was an "earthly paradise" and a favorite holiday resort for wealthy South Africans from Durban and Johannesburg, did little to dispel the alarm of the royal party. They believed that the shah, like Napoleon at St. Helena, was to be exiled, along with his family, to a remote island in the middle of nowhere, and among "lions and crocodiles" to boot.[48]

When Skrine returned to the *Bandra* that evening, however, he found the mood more resigned, or at least stoic—although the young princes took to spitting overboard in unison, whenever a British-Indian navy patrol boat passed by.[49] The family set about learning as much about the island as they could; Princess Shams could think only of the "mournful" Mauritius she had encountered when studying French in the novel, *Paul et Virginie,* by Bernard de St. Pierre, which was set on the island.[50]

Skrine had been charged with obtaining, in Bombay, the linen, mattresses, carpeting, and other items that the governor of Mauritius advised the royal party bring with them. He now found himself saddled with an additional assignment. Members of the royal family had brought little baggage with them, had no clothes suitable to a tropical climate, and had been expecting to shop in Bombay. The shopping now fell to Skrine, and the list proved extensive. Reza Shah, having purchased three Persian carpets in Kerman, wanted another four large Persian rugs:

> The men and boys wanted suits, shirts, haberdashery of all kinds, shoes, bedding, watches, cameras, toilet articles … while the ladies craved whole trousseaus, including vast quantities of lingerie … One Prince wanted a sixteen millimetre cine-camera and projection outfit, another the best binoculars money could buy, a third, tennis-racquets and a Leica camera … The Senior Princess instructed me to find for her a two-seater sports car.[51]

Skrine secured most of these items at the Bombay army and navy store. "After a long search" he also found four Kerman rugs for Reza Shah and "after ransacking the car-shops" a two-seater Sunbeam Talbot sports car for Princess Shams. He also purchased, as requested, two refrigerators, gold watches for the ladies, and a number of other luxury items. He drove the Sunbeam Talbot on board the ship himself. However, to Skrine's dismay, Princess Shams was not impressed. She found the Sunbeam Talbot insufficiently streamlined, and she disliked its crushed strawberry color.[52] Skrine, instructed to keep secret Reza Shah's presence on the *Bandra* off the Indian coast, decided he could trust the discretion of the army and navy store manager's English tailor to take measurements and sew clothes for the men. A friend put him in touch with a Mrs. Jenkins, a young woman of Mauritian extraction who was married to a British port official. He took her on board with him as well. The tailor "was soon busy with tape and pencil … [and] covered at least a dozen sheets of paper with orders and measurements," Skrine wrote, while Mrs. Jenkins was a great hit with the princesses. She spoke French as they did, was able to advise them on what to take with them to Mauritius, and to answer many questions about life on the island.[53]

The family remained at Bombay port for five days, although family and baggage were transferred to the SS *Burma*, which pulled alongside the *Bandra* on the third day, for the onward journey to Mauritius. The FO, the CO, and Governor Bede in Mauritius were already making arrangements for Reza Shah's arrival. Bede's staff found and furnished a suitable residence; and in London British officials began putting in place the regime that would govern Reza Shah's stay on the island. Still concerned lest Reza Shah become the focus of "intrigue" by Britain's enemies or initiate such intrigue himself (concerns that proved totally unfounded), British officials established parameters regulating the freedom the royal family would be allowed, the forms of "discreet" supervision that would be exercised over them, and the type of censorship that would be conducted over correspondence between the royal family in Mauritius and the palace and relatives in Tehran.

The *Burma* sailed from Bombay on October 6 and arrived at Mauritius on October 18. Even the difficult-to-please Princess Shams described the island, seen from the deck of the ship, as "Eden-like ... verdant ... full of flowers."[54] Reza Shah, however, found the island oppressive. His exile had begun.

5

Mauritius: "This Is a Prison ... a Death in Life"

In exile, Reza Shah was no longer a free man. The conditions of his exile were dictated not by himself but by the British; and the relationship between the two remained uneasy. Britain's handling of Reza Shah—the degree and freedom and choice they were prepared to allow him and his family—was dictated by what for them were the exigencies of war. Throughout the exile, they felt they were dealing with a difficult man and a difficult, demanding, and tiresome family. Unable to free himself entirely from the bonds of British control, Reza Shah sought to at least loosen these bonds, to make his own choices as to where and how to live, and to maintain his dignity under what he regarded as undignified conditions. In Tehran, his son and successor, Mohammad Reza Shah, also played a role. He used what leverage he had with the British to help ease the conditions of his father's exile, even as he endeavored to satisfy Allied demands and protect Iran's interests under a difficult foreign occupation. The push and pull of cross-purposes entailed by this triangular relationship defined Reza Shah's life in exile in both Mauritius and Johannesburg.

Britain and Their Difficult Guest

In managing Reza Shah's exile, Britain pursued two not always compatible goals. On the one hand, they did not want on their hands an unhappy ex-king and family; and they needed the goodwill and cooperation of the new shah and his government in Tehran for the war effort. Large numbers of occupying British and Soviet troops had to be accommodated; remaining German nationals and suspected German agents and sympathizers had to be rounded up; and, most important, the Allies required Iranian cooperation to ensure unimpeded use of the Iranian road, rail, and port network to move massive supplies and weaponry to a hard-pressed Soviet Union. This meant keeping Reza Shah and the royal family reasonably comfortable and content, meeting their requirements and requests, keeping the older boys occupied and out of trouble, and ensuring that Mohammad Reza Shah was satisfied that his father was being treated well. On the other hand, the British were concerned lest Reza Shah become the target of Nazi intrigue or engage in intrigue himself; and they did not want his presence in exile to attract press attention that would reflect unfavorably on Great Britain. This required keeping Reza Shah firmly in British hands somewhere in the British Empire, and exercising what they described as a "discreet surveillance" over his movements and activities, censoring his mail, controlling the visitors he could receive, even from members of his own family from Iran, and restricting travel by his sons and daughters outside Mauritius and, later, Johannesburg. There were also the practical problems of finding and furnishing suitable housing for the ex-shah and his large family and arranging for day-to-day household maintenance and servants. Later, in South Africa, there was the sensitive problem of the color bar; and even in Mauritius the governor, Bede Clifford, faced a delicate task in handling relations between the Mauritian elite and the unwanted guests in their midst.

The need to address these issues was initially prompted by Clifford's request for guidance as to how he should handle Reza Shah and his large party. After some back and forth between Mauritius, the Colonial Office, and the Foreign Office, Clifford was issued guidelines that, although modified from time to time, governed the British handling of Reza Shah in exile until his death in 1944. When Mauritius was chosen as his place of exile, the secretary of state for the colonies informed Clifford in a cable,

> The decision to send [Reza Shah] to Mauritius is based on the requirements of the war situation; and … there is no intention of treating him as a prisoner in Mauritius, where every consideration will be shown to him and every effort will be made to render his stay as agreeable as possible. It is therefore desirable that he should be afforded all reasonable facilities and freedom of movement.[1]

However,

> In the event of ex-Shah or members of his household attempting to cause political or other trouble in the Colony, you have full discretion to restrict their freedom of movement by any means.[2] It is only proposed that a discreet

surveillance (e.g. by gardeners, etc.) sh[oul]d be exercised, so the ex-Shah sh[oul]d not feel slighted.[3]

Clifford went out of his way to make the ex-shah feel welcome in Mauritius. His staff located a suitable residence in one of the best neighborhoods, Moka, in the capital city of Port Louis, not far from Government House. The residence, Valory, was a fine, three-story villa, with enough rooms to accommodate the royal family. The garden was extensive, with many trees, a swimming pool, and a stream running through it. The younger boys and the royal secretary were housed in a smaller bungalow, and some of the staff in an annex, on the ample grounds. A nearby house was later found for the Shah's oldest daughter, Princess Shams, who wanted a separate residence for herself and her husband. (This entailed delicate persuasion according to Clarmont Skrine, the political officer with the Government of India assigned to accompany Reza Shah to Mauritius. The owners, he wrote, "French Mauritanians of good family do not want to move.")[4] Clifford's wife, Alice, furnished the main house with Empire furniture she found in the Port Louis museum. The furniture, including a magnificent four-poster bed, belonged to Napoleon's general Charles Matthiue Isadore Decaen, the governor of Mauritius when the island was under French rule. Alice Clifford and Skrine were especially proud of the bed, whose headboard they decorated with a royal crown; around it they hung lace curtains. To their disappointment, Reza Shah refused the bed and, as was his habit, slept on a rug on the floor.

Clifford assigned a government research physician, H. D. Tonking, to serve as principal aide to Reza Shah; and the head of the department of public works took care of staffing the house, gardening, and transport. He named a junior official, Monsieur Valet, to take family members shopping and sightseeing and to see to their other needs; and Clifford put the island's most expensive French-style caterers in charge of meals and the kitchen and asked the island's best doctors to look after the family's health. When the SS *Burma*, the ship that carried the royal family from Bombay port to Mauritius, docked at Port Louis, Clifford went on board in full dress uniform to greet the ex-shah; on shore, he placed an honor guard of two companies of territorial infantry. When the royal party arrived at Valory, the Iranian tricolored flag, emblazoned with the lion and sun, fluttered above the main house. The flag had been sewn by Alice Clifford and lady friends, using a color photograph they found in a magazine.[5]

Censorship and Travel Restrictions

Clifford, in two successive telegrams, had also urgently requested guidance on censorship.[6] The question was addressed in correspondence between the Government of India, the FO, and the Colonial Office; and officials decided that correspondence from the palace and others in Iran to Reza Shah and his party could be freely passed; but that all correspondence from Mauritius to Tehran should be subject to censorship. The head of the eastern department at the FO, C. W. Baxter, summarized the consensus view: "It does not seem to make much difference to us what people write to the ex-Shah and his party. Provided that the letters from the ex-Shah and party are censored, I do not think we need bother about correspondence going in the reverse direction."[7] The arrangement put in place required Skrine, who read Persian, to examine all correspondence emanating from Mauritius, to prepare summary translations for the Mauritian authorities, and to censor whatever he thought necessary. The letters were then sent to Cairo where they were subject to a further examination by the Anglo-Egyptian censor's office before being forwarded to Tehran. Governor Clifford informed Reza Shah in general of these arrangements: correspondence in English or French, he told him, would be locally censored; correspondence in Persian would be sent to the Cairo censorship office.[8]

Censorship came into play even before the royal family arrived in Mauritius. Reza Shah had reacted in anger when he learned, while on the SS *Bandra* at Bombay port waiting to disembark on his way to Argentina, that he would not be allowed to land in India and was being sent into exile to Mauritius. His son, Prince Ali Reza, sent off letters to the ruling shah and other family members in Tehran. The letters, the Government of India noted,

> accuse British of breach of faith and contain extravagant phrases such as "the English have played their traditional trick of St. Helena and Napoleon," "Indian and English soldiers took us into custody," "failing Divine intervention my father will probably become a slave to these people … the life of everyone of us is in danger."[9]

These letters were intercepted and not allowed to pass, as was up a follow-up telegram from the prince to the shah, in which he reported that they had been "tricked, were virtual prisoners in Mauritius, disliked the island intensely and were anxious to go elsewhere."[10] "Ali Reza is the most unpleasant of all the ex-Shah's sons and one w[oul]d expect him to write in this strain," commented I. T. M. Pink, an officer dealing with Iran at the FO.[11]

British officials remained exercised throughout Reza Shah's stay in Mauritius that no note of discontent with the conditions on the island reach the palace in Tehran. When Skrine left Mauritius after five weeks with the royal party, he carried with him a batch of some thirty-five letters from members of the royal party to relatives and friends in Iran. He reviewed these letters with a member of the Anglo-Egyptian censor's office during a stopover in Cairo. Skrine let through several letters he described as "quite harmless" or "quite reasonable and harmless." On the other hand, he censored all letters critical of conditions in which the royal party found themselves in Mauritius. For example, he described letters from Princess Shams to relatives and friends in Tehran as "emotional, querulous and exaggerated and have been held up being likely to cause despondency and alarm in Tehran"; and of a letter by one of Reza Shah's sons to the ruling shah in Iran, he wrote, "highly emotional and exaggerated and has been held up."[12] Clifford reported he was on his own allowing through only letters "containing family greetings and requests for money."[13] Later, letters were sometimes not passed due to the need for secrecy and to avoid public knowledge of Reza Shah's movements or whereabouts.[14]

Once in Mauritius, Reza Shah was safely beyond the reach of German or enemy agents, as the British intended. But, as noted, FO and Colonial Office officials were concerned (with no reason, as it turned out) lest Reza Shah cause them problems. On the eve of Reza Shah's arrival in Mauritius, A. B. Acheson of the Colonial Office noted, "There are in Mauritius some 40,000–50,000 Moslems among whom the ex-Shah might attempt to cause trouble. And he might obtain some help from the small but influential pro-Vichy element among the Franco-Mauritians. In that event, it might be necessary for the Governor to take firm action."[15] On Mauritius, there was another exile, Milan Stoyadinovitch, a Serbian nationalist and former Yugoslav finance and prime minister. The British had taken him into exile at the request of the Yugoslav prince regent, Paul, who feared Stoyadinovich, then out of office, would cooperate in a pro-Axis coup. British officials even worried that Reza Shah and Stoyadinovich might meet. "It may be safer for the ex-Shah and Stoyadinovich not to get together," Pink at the FO commented. However, British officials concluded that they need not bar a meeting, as long as Reza Shah understood that Stoyadinovich was allowed to meet only with approved persons and only with a guard listening.[16]

These broad concerns provided the basis for the instructions issued to Clifford: Reza Shah and his party "would have to be kept under observation but not necessarily closely guarded"[17] and, as already noted, Clifford was authorized to restrict their movements and meetings with others, if this proved necessary.

At the same time, British officials took care that the royal party not feel slighted, especially since Skrine had reported that the ex-shah and his sons "really thought at first that they were going to be treated as prisoners of war," and that they would be "under guard or surveillance" in Mauritius, a situation, he wrote, touching on "their *amour propre* more than anything else."[18] Clifford was so informed and, in response, he wrote to the secretary of state for the colonies:

> I do not propose to insist on plain clothes chauffeurs and the like, mentioned in my [earlier] telegram, if they are objected to, and will confine observation measures to placing intelligent and reliable Mohammedan and Sikh Punjabi warders in charge of convict gardeners, with instructions to report anything unusual, particularly as regards visitors and outside contacts.[19]

All these precautions proved unnecessary. Reza Shah displayed no interest in engaging in "intrigue" or "causing trouble" among the Muslim community in Mauritius. He never met with Stoyadinovich and probably wasn't even aware of his existence. He had no contact with the Vichy element among the Franco-Mauritian community. All he wanted was to be left alone. In his seven months in Mauritius, but for two occasions, he never even ventured out of Valory, restricting himself to walking in its gardens.

On the island itself, Reza Shah and his family were allowed full freedom of movement; but leaving Mauritius remained subject to British acquiescence. Reza Shah, as noted, had left Iran accompanied by nineteen others—his wife, Esmat, her stepsister, Qamar Mobasher, and a lady-in-waiting, Behjat Moshar, six sons and two daughters, a private secretary and his son-in-law, a cook, and several servants. Not long after arrival in Mauritius the queen's stepsister and the lady-in-waiting grew impatient to return to Iran. Reza Shah's eldest daughter, Princess Shams; her husband, Fereydoun Jam; and Reza Shah's personal secretary, Ali Izadi, desired to travel elsewhere—to a neutral country or to another part of the British Empire. Governor Clifford would have been happy to see Princess Shams off the island. Skrine had written of the princess that "she is about the most selfish and spoilt young woman I have ever met, but being a great favorite with the ex-Shah her nuisance value is considerable."[20] Clifford, more circumspect, described her as "the most restless member of the party," adding that "her temporary absence will conduce to greater contentment among the others."[21]

British officials permitted the queen's stepsister and the lady-in waiting to return home but decided that Shams—"by all accounts an extremely tiresome young woman"[22] —her husband, Jam, and Izadi should stay put. (As it turned out, only the queen's stepsister went home; the lady-in-waiting decided to stay). These restrictions on Reza Shah and all members of his family remained in force for several months, when circumstances changed and the British finally relented.

Napoleon at Elba?

Mauritius was hardly an unattractive place. When Skrine first informed an angry Reza Shah on board the SS *Bandra*, at Bombay, that he would be going into exile to Mauritius rather than to a country of his own choosing, he assured the royal family, as we have seen, that Mauritius was a highly attractive place in which to live.[23] He was not seeking merely to assuage the alarms of the family, who feared that they would be living among "malarial swamps, lions and crocodiles" off the African coast. Skrine was charmed by the island himself. He remarked on its "gardens gay with geranium and bougainvillea," its Riviera-like climate, and its many beauty spots along sea and mountain. The governor's residence, Le Reduit, he wrote, was "an eighteenth-century French chateau, all dazzling white colonnades and loggias festooned with begonias and clematis … surely unsurpassed in the Empire for the beauty of its surroundings and the grace of its architecture." "My meat," he later wrote, "was certainly Mauritius."[24]

Princess Shams noted much to admire about the island: the abundance of flowers, especially the bougainvillea beloved by Iranians; the many fine homes and villas, with their greenery-covered walls and gardens; the public parks; and playing fields. "All in all," she wrote, "a small, European city."[25] The residence, Valory, she remarked, had ample rooms, the garden was extensive and rich in trees and greenery, the swimming pool was "as large as a small lake," the number of servants adequate, and those in charge of the help dedicated and committed to good service. The British proved to be generous hosts and "made available everything we needed for our material comfort."[26]

Yet Mauritius was not entirely to the royal family's liking. They had arrived at the beginning of the hot season, and Princess Shams wrote of the dampness, the intense, almost unbearable heat, the heavy downpours—it sometimes rained seven or eight hours a day—and of the flying ants that were everywhere and covered the washbasins and bathtubs in the morning.[27] The queen remembered the large lizards that fell down from trees even as she was walking with Reza Shah in the garden at Valory.[28] Distance and censorship meant letters to and from Iran were infrequent. It sometimes took weeks for letters to arrive and, due to censorship, family members felt unable to write freely as to what was truly in their hearts regarding life on Mauritius.[29]

Shams recalled that her only entertainment was bicycling several hours a day, movies, studying Italian, and the piano lessons she resumed once a teacher could be found.[30] The boys also reported they did not have enough to do. Reza Shah had insisted that his sons engage in physical exercise and continue their studies. They worked with a private trainer and took lessons in English, French, and other subjects from a tutor. But Prince Ali Reza wrote dismissively of Mauritius in a letter to his cousin in Tehran. The sports available on the island paled in comparison to those they had enjoyed at home; a private tutor was not the same as going to a real school; the available hunting—of rabbits, bats, and deer—did not measure up to the hunting in Iran either; and the absence of horses meant the boys couldn't go riding. Lessons and exercise aside, there were only movies and occasional outings to the cooler environs of Curepipe, along the mountains above Port Louis. Out of boredom, the 20-year-old prince wrote that he had taken to smoking three or four cigarettes a day.[31] Clifford, somewhat less charitably, reported that the boys were "disappointed at the absence of theatres and cabarets" and with Mauritius as a holiday resort.[32]

Members of Mauritian society did not exactly welcome the newcomers. The island's small population consisted primarily of native Mauritians, mostly Creoles of African ancestry, a large community of Muslim Indians engaged in various trades, and a smaller community of Europeans—French families whose forebears came when the French controlled the island and British military personnel and government officials. Clifford reported that he had asked the officer commanding British troops to offer members of the royal family the social amenities of the military club and "though I have requested the leading members of local society to help make their stay here agreeable, the parties are so temperamentally incompatible that I anticipate there will be little cordiality between them."[33] Along the same lines, Skrine reported that

> the French Mauritians who form the large majority of the European community are already inclined to resent the presence of the ex-Shah and party on the island. There is a very strong color-bar here and I regret to say that in spite of the strong lead given by Sir Bede and Lady Clifford, Mauritian society (outside of the small British official and military circle) does not seem inclined to show friendliness to the Persians or to put itself out in any way on their behalf.[34]

Not surprisingly, the feeling among Reza Shah's sons and daughters that they had ended up in the middle of nowhere persisted. According to Princess Shams, Reza Shah in any case discouraged his children from mixing with the Europeans.[35]

Reza Shah intensely disliked Mauritius. The hot, damp climate did not suit him; he yearned, he said, for the cool, bracing air of his homeland. He complained that he slept badly and that the croaking of the frogs, who seemed everywhere at Valory, kept him awake at night, so much so that the servants were sent out to try and collect them.[36] He was greatly upset by unfavorable and disparaging comments in the local press when representatives of the Muslim community called on him on his arrival in Mauritius.[37] "His detention on a small mid-ocean island," Clifford noted in a cable, "creates unwarranted and unalterable impression that he is a prisoner ... and he suffers accordingly in his pride and *amour propre*."[38] Visibly despondent, he avoided contact with anyone outside the family and spent a great deal of the day walking in the garden at Valory. The family, unwilling to leave him by himself, arranged for one of them to accompany him always.[39] As was his lifetime habit, he established for himself a routine to which he strictly adhered, down to the time of the day he smoked his first cigarette, had his mid-morning and afternoon tea, and ate his meals. As always, he rose early, usually at five in the morning, had his breakfast, and then walked for a good two hours. After lunch with the family, he walked again—and once again in the evening. Clifford and other Mauritian officials remarked on his penchant for "vigorous exercise."

Eager for news from Iran he spent the evenings with the rest of the family around the radio. One of his sons was charged with dialing to the news broadcasts from Radio Tehran and the Persian-language broadcasts of the BBC and Radio Berlin. This often proved a frustrating business, as reception, especially of Radio Tehran, was poor. Knowing of his hunger for news of Iran and the war, Jam and others in the family often had to piece together the bits of news they could pick up from various scratchy broadcasts and bring their reports to him. Over lunch or dinner he would reminisce at length on his life as a soldier and as king. Jam asked for permission to put down on paper Reza Shah's reminiscences. He refused. He would dictate his memoirs for Jam to write down once he was settled elsewhere, outside Mauritius, he said. He wanted the memoir to reflect his own words—precisely. (The memoirs were never written.)

He was similarly exacting in the letters he wrote to the British authorities objecting to his incarceration in Mauritius. He dictated the letters to Jam in Persian; Jam translated the letters into French. Before the letters could be handed over to the British, Jam had to translate them back into Persian for his father-in-law. Reza Shah would then have one of his sons do same thing— all this to ensure that his own exact words had been conveyed to the British. He also bore, in exile, what seemed to him the ignominy of wearing civilian clothes. This was a "punishment" he imposed on himself. As king, he had always dressed in the military uniform he had worn as a soldier. Once he gave up the throne, he somehow felt he must give up military dress as well. Yet he hated wearing civilian clothes. Jam pointed out that Napoleon had continued to wear his military uniform during his exile on the island of St. Helena, but to no avail.

When Reza Shah first heard from Skrine while on the SS *Burma* at Bombay that the British were sending him to Mauritius, he had cabled the viceroy of India that he had been "arrested"; and he told Skrine he would never have agreed to leave Iran had he known "he was to be made a prisoner of war."[40] The insistence that he was not a free man (and he wasn't) and now a prisoner persisted throughout the Mauritius period. "I am a prisoner and must behave like a prisoner," he told his son-in-law, Jam.[41] In conversation with Clifford, he conceded that he was allowed full freedom of movement on the island, but he still regarded himself as a prisoner. When Clifford, at tea with Reza Shah after he was settled at Valory, asked him whether he was comfortable and receiving all the attention he required, he replied, "What shall I say? We are prisoners ... Mauritius is a prison, albeit a big one. We are accustomed to great open spaces and mountains to which to escape the heat. To us this existence is unreal—a sort of death in life."[42] The shah, Clifford wrote in his memoirs, "never became reconciled to his detention in Mauritius."[43]

To underline he was a prisoner, and despite pleading by his sons and daughters that he join them for an outing to a movie or elsewhere, he refused to leave the Valory compound, "imposing on himself," as one British official put it, "a voluntary imprisonment."[44] He left the house only on two occasions. The first time, he rushed to the scene of a car accident involving one of his sons and his private secretary, Ali Izadi. (Izadi was badly injured, the son was not.) The second time he attended a black-tie dinner Clifford gave to mark the signing of the Tripartite Agreement between Iran, Britain, and the Soviet Union in January 1942. Even then, Reza Shah did not join the rest of the family for the entire evening. His son-in-law went from the governor's mansion to pick him up only after the formal dinner. He found Reza Shah seated on the bed in his room, partially and uncomfortably dressed in the formal black tie suit that had been sewn for him during the stopover offshore in Bombay. He had the bow tie in his hand: "May God grant me death," he told his son-in-law. "What is this harness I must wear around my neck?" Jam knotted the bow tie on for him and drove him to the governor's house. He remained ten minutes and Jam then drove him back to Valory.[45]

It was perhaps inevitable that Reza Shah's exile in Mauritius should conjure up for both the English and the Iranians Napoleon's exile on the islands of Elba and St. Helena. In the letter he dispatched to the ruling shah in Tehran when the royal party first learned they would have to go to Mauritius, Prince

Ali Reza, as noted, wrote that "the British have played their traditional trick of St. Helena and Napoleon."[46] Reader Bullard, the British minister in Tehran, bristled at this comparison.

> It is typical of this base people that the ex-Shah is now becoming popular again as the alleged victim of British cruelty … it flatters the Persian to compare the ex-Shah with Napoleon and makes him feel less ignoble to believe that the ruler whose slave he was for so long, was a great man.[47]

In fact, the British savored the Napoleon trope themselves. Skrine wrote, tongue in cheek, that his mission was "to play Sir Hudson Low [the British governor of St. Helena when Napoleon was exiled there] to Reza Shah's Napoleon."[48] At the conclusion of his mission and after saying farewell to Reza Shah, Skrine noted, "Here, I leave the Napoleon of modern Persia upon his fairer St. Helena."[49] Having fitted out Reza Shah's house in Mauritius with furniture that had belonged to Napoleon's general, Clifford found "the association between Napoleon on St. Helena and the Shah in Mauritius surrounded by Empire furniture … singularly fortuitous and appropriate."[50] But Reza Shah did not share these sentiments. He found the comparison between himself and Napoleon "humiliating rather than complimentary," Clifford noted.[51]

The Tripartite Treaty

From the moment he arrived on Mauritius, Reza Shah pressed to go elsewhere: to Canada, South Africa, America, Argentina. In letters or cables to the ruling shah, he urged his son to raise the matter with the British minister in Tehran. In informal meetings and formal interviews with Clifford, he asked the governor, and also asked Skrine, to raise the matter with their superiors. On instructions from Tehran, the Iranian minister in London, Hassan Taqizadeh, spoke to officials at the FO. Reza Shah made his own case to Clifford: since the outbreak of the war, he said, he had at no time acted against the interests of Great Britain or in favor of Germany. He had sought only to adhere to strict neutrality. Had the British taken him into their confidence regarding Allied strategic requirements, he would have been ready to negotiate; and, having abdicated "to facilitate [Britain's] plans" and having admitted British troops into his country without opposition, he should be treated as an ally, not a prisoner, and be allowed to settle in a neutral country.[52]

British officials remained unsympathetic. A move entailed considerable costs and extensive arrangements—transport for a large party in a time of war, agreement from officials in another part of the British Empire to house the ex-shah and his extended family, security safeguards in the new location. Yet they could not ignore the ex-shah's wishes, either. His health might deteriorate as he grew more despondent. The shah in Tehran was pressing his father's case; and the British needed Mohammad Reza Shah's cooperation. The Tripartite Treaty with Iran was still under negotiation and the British were anxious to nail it down.

A word on the Tripartite Treaty: having entered Iran not by invitation but as an occupying force, Britain and the Soviet Union were anxious to place the presence of their forces on Iranian soil on a more friendly and secure footing. This required formal Iranian agreement and Iranian support for a military presence that would certainly continue until the end of the war. The negotiations over a treaty proved difficult, however. Iran had demands and concerns of her own and bargained hard to secure them. When Prime Minister Mohammad Ali Foroughi presented to the Majlis an agreement that he believed protected Iranian interests, deputies objected that Iran was giving up too much and receiving back too little. In exasperation, Harold Caccia at the FO commented that "the Persian democratic method looks like becoming a Frankenstein monster."[53] The fate of Reza Shah became tied up with these difficult negotiations.

In late October 1941, Bullard cabled the FO from Tehran that the shah was anxious about his father and asked whether Reza Shah and his family could go to Argentina. Bullard requested guidance as to how to reply.[54] His cable prompted a flurry of exchanges among FO officials. Pink tentatively broached the idea of allowing Reza Shah to go, not to Argentina or a neutral country where he might become "the center of Axis intrigue," and where "we should have no control over him," but perhaps to Canada, South Africa, or even the United States. While the advantages of leaving him in Mauritius were obvious, he wrote, "it is possible that in the long run we should benefit from a more generous policy." Harold Caccia, the deputy undersecretary, disagreed: "We are not under any obligation, moral or contractual, expressed or implied, in this matter," he wrote. "I do not see that we have anything much to gain from moving him and his family nearer 'theatres and cabarets.'" Reza Shah's argument, that he had abdicated to facilitate British plans and should now be allowed to retire to a neutral country, Caccia added, was equivalent to the claim of a prisoner for clemency for having pleaded guilty. "The judge is under no obligation to let him off hard labor because he saved the Crown the trouble of a long case." Harold Seymour, the assistant undersecretary for the Middle East and the Far East, observed that "the Ex-Shah and his family would be a nuisance anywhere," but recommended they be kept in Mauritius for the duration of the war. The shah in Tehran could in the meantime be told that the situation would be reviewed in one year.[55] Seymour's view prevailed; the Government of India concurred; and Bullard was instructed to so inform the shah. The royal party would stay in Mauritius for the war's duration, but their status could be reconsidered in one year's time.

This did not end the matter. Bullard cabled two weeks later that the shah in Tehran asked, since Argentina had been ruled out, if Reza Shah and the family could go to Canada, where the family would be more content and the boys could be educated. In mid-November, the shah enquired if Bullard had received a reply from London, stressing that Reza Shah could not be the target of Axis intrigue in Canada.[56] At the same time, Clifford cabled from Mauritius on November 13 that Reza Shah's eldest son in Mauritius, Ali Reza, had come to see him. The prince reported that his father was very despondent and that he was genuinely concerned for Reza Shah's mental and physical health, given his advanced age. Ali Reza believed the main problem was uncertainty: his father could face another three or even six months in Mauritius, as long as a date for departure were fixed and he had something to look forward to.[57] Clifford expressed his own concern: Reza Shah was showing signs of "increasing restiveness"; a breakdown in his health could result in "unpleasant political consequences."[58] He recommended the ex-shah be promised transfer elsewhere on the conclusion of the Tripartite Treaty or within a definite period of time.

These new communications had an effect. The foreign secretary, Anthony Eden, grew ready to allow Reza Shah to relocate, but with a condition. On the margins of Clifford's cable, Eden wrote in his trademark red ink: "Could we not say we will try to arrange something once the [Tripartite] Treaty is signed?"

Pink added that there were advantages to allowing Reza Shah to go to Canada "if we could make use of him as a pawn in our treaty negotiations ... We want above all to be rid of him as a political problem." At Eden's instructions, the FO asked the Dominions Office to persuade the Canadian government to harbor the ex-Shah for the duration of the war.[59]

In a detailed letter to Eric Machtig, his counterpart at the Dominions Office, Alexander Cadogan, the permanent undersecretary at the FO, explained the situation: Reza Shah was unhappy in Mauritius; he had wanted to go to Argentina or elsewhere, but His Majesty's Government (HMG) had demurred out of concern he might be exploited to Britain's disadvantage. The ex-shah now wanted to go to Canada, where the climate was similar to the Iranian uplands, the amenities better, and where his sons could be educated. There were disadvantages in keeping him in Mauritius against his will, Cadogan added, and "the present Shah's willingness to cooperate with us may depend to a considerable extent on whether he is convinced his father is being fairly treated." Caccia then asked if Canada would accept Reza Shah for the duration of the war. The FO, he explained, was imposing this burden on the Government of Canada only due to the "necessities of the war situation." In language that echoed the instructions issued to Clifford when Reza Shah was being sent to Mauritius, Cadogan added that the burden would not be too onerous: Reza Shah and his family were not to be treated as prisoners in any way "though of course, they should not be allowed to leave Canada ... and it would only be necessary to exercise a discreet surveillance over their movement and political contacts and to censor their correspondence. As to finance, arrangements would of course be made that no burden would fall on Canadian funds."[60]

In a long cable the following day, Eden informed Bullard in confidence that the FO was taking steps to ascertain whether Reza Shah could be sent elsewhere. However, "you should for the present show the Persian authorities that we are not prepared to be agreeable about anything until the Treaty is signed and has entered into force." Bullard was authorized to tell the ruling shah only that H. M. G. "will be ready to review the situation from time to time"; and he could supplement this official reply "with a personal statement as from yourself that you have reason to believe that His Majesty's Government will be prepared, as soon as the Treaty is signed, to see whether arrangements can be made to transfer the ex-Shah to some other part of the empire."[61]

Mohammad Reza Shah, taking all this in, commented ruefully that it was hard that Reza Shah's transfer from Mauritius should depend on the signature of the treaty, as he had done his best throughout the negotiations to expedite it.[62]

The Canadian government agreed to accept Reza Shah and his sons. The Tripartite Treaty was approved by the Majlis on January 26, 1942, and was formally signed by the representatives of the three countries three days later. Under the terms of the treaty, Iran undertook to allow the Allies the unrestricted right to use, maintain, and, if necessary, to control all means of communication throughout Iran (which was understood to apply to the road and rail network, seaports, and airfields); to establish measures of censorship of all communications in cooperation with the Allies; to assist in providing labor and material to maintain and improve communication networks; and to adopt a foreign policy friendly to the war aims of the Allies. Britain and the Soviet Union, for their part, undertook to respect the independence and territorial integrity of Iran and to withdraw Allied forces from Iran within six months of the end of all hostilities.[63]

Both Reza Shah and the ruling shah in Tehran were now officially informed that Reza Shah could proceed to Canada. In Mauritius, Princess Shams detected a marked change in British behavior toward the royal family. "A gentle breeze," she wrote, wafted from the British side. Letters arrived and were accepted more regularly and limitations on the royal family considerably eased.[64]

To Canada—or to South Africa?

Anticipating treaty signature, the FO and the Colonial Office began in late December to prepare for the transfer of the ex-shah and his party to Canada. They also decided to allow those members of the royal family who so desired to return to Iran. Shams and her husband were eager to return, as was the queen and the lady-in-waiting, Behjat Moshar. All of the Iranian servants, except one, wished to go home too. Reza Shah's private secretary, Ali Izadi, agreed to remain until a replacement was sent from Iran. The ex-shah decided to send home with their mother his youngest son and daughter, aged 9 and 14, but to take his five older sons with him to Canada. The logistics in a time of war proved complicated. Both those going to Canada and those returning to

Iran had to sail first to Durban, South Africa. Passage for the whole party from Mauritius to Durban and from there to Canada and Iran had to be arranged through the Ministry of War Transport and Sea Transport officers at Durban and Bombay. Shams, impatient to depart, did not wait for her father. She left Mauritius with her husband and the eight others headed for Iran on February 20 on the Dutch passenger ship, the KPM *Tegelberg*. They arrived in Durban five days later.

Shams and Jam wished to avoid a long sea voyage from Durban to Bombay, and the British had arranged for the couple to fly from Durban to Cairo and from there to Tehran; but due to a mix-up the couple ended up joining the rest of the party on a ship to Mombasa, Kenya, a major British naval base during the war. Due to Shams's illness, she and Jam disembarked there and, after a three-day wait, they flew from Mombasa to Cairo and Tehran. It is a measure of the persistently uneasy relationship between the Iranians and the British that, according to Princess Shams, a British officer showed up at her hotel room in Mombasa to report that she and her husband would not be allowed out of the hotel. The restriction was lifted only after she telegraphed the Iranian ambassador in Cairo to ask King Farouk to intercede with the British authorities on her behalf.[65] (Mohammad Reza Shah's wife was King Farouk's sister.) The rest of the party continued by sea to Bombay. From there, the queen and the two children returned home overland by rail and automobile; the others took the sea route.

As Shams and others made their way home, British officials remained anxious to avoid negative reports regarding the royal family's stay in Mauritius. Anticipating Princess Shams's arrival in Bombay, Governor Clifford cabled to the Colonial Office: "I suggest that, on their arrival in Bombay, every consideration should be shown to Princess Shams and the party. If carefully approached, it should be possible to induce them to permit us to announce that, apart from their objection to going and staying in Mauritius, they received every consideration."[66] At the FO, W. H. Young also hoped to avoid negative publicity regarding the "alleged unpleasantness" of the royal family's Mauritius experience; but he thought such publicity inevitable. "The party will in any case tell the wildest stories as soon as they get back to Persia," he wrote.[67] He was not far wrong. Bullard cabled a short while later that that he had received a personal message from the shah: Shams and Jam were back in Tehran and reported that they had been treated as "undesirable aliens rather than as allies" in Mauritius.[68]

Reza Shah's own departure was delayed, initially due to a "servant problem," then because he fell ill. A new batch of servants to replace those returning home and a replacement private secretary were ready to set sail from Iran. But their arrival in Mauritius or, alternatively, South Africa would take many weeks, and Reza Shah was reluctant to go further than Durban without servants. This was also the British view: "We can hardly send the ex-Shah's party on to South Africa and Canada without servants," Young at the FO observed.[69] The FO seemed to welcome the delay. "We are at present in no hurry to move the ex-Shah," Young remarked on February 22.[70] A day later, noting that Eden wanted to be consulted before Reza Shah was allowed to leave Mauritius, he added, "The servant problem has provided a useful excuse for keeping the ex-Shah in Mauritius for the time being."[71]

Servants or no servants, Reza Shah remained impatient to leave. "Ex-Shah is growing very restive and thinks we are trifling with him." Clifford cabled from Mauritius two weeks later. "They are ready to travel by tramp steamer and pay their own way,"[72] but only a "rather dirty tramp" was immediately available. At the FO, H. A. Caccia dryly remarked, "We must, if possible, avoid the ex-Shah travelling on a rather dirty tramp."[73]

The ex-shah, however, fell seriously ill on the eve of his departure. Doctors diagnosed cardiac failure, liver disease, and intestinal problems. They feared a growth in his abdomen might be malignant (this later proved not to be the case).[74] The British felt they had a crisis on their hands—Reza Shah might die—and they set about preparing for the worst. The British ambassador in Tehran, Sir Reader Bullard, was instructed to inform the ruling shah that his father was dangerously ill and that his condition was deteriorating. Given that Reza Shah had objected to Mauritius in the first place, the governor, Bede Clifford, cabled to the secretary of state for the colonies that "it would seem politically advisable to get him away just as soon as possible." In a second cable, he emphasized that "every effort should be made to get him out of Mauritius alive."[75] In London, officials at the FO concurred. If the ex-shah recovered sufficiently and could be moved, observed W. H. Young, one of the FO officials dealing with Iran, "we shall, I think, have to get him out of Mauritius as soon as possible." Young added,

If the ex-Shah dies and an announcement is made suddenly and without any previous preparation, all sorts of rumors are likely to get about in Persia, including the accusation that H. M. G. have murdered him or at any rate hastened his death. No amount of denials ever succeed in laying [to rest] stories of this kind.[76]

After some back and forth at the FO, rather than have the BBC Persian service—an official source—broadcast news of the ex-shah's illness and risk, as one official put it, that "the Persians might put it out just in the wrong way,"[77] officials decided to first have the *Times* report that Reza Shah's health was a cause for anxiety and then have the BBC broadcast the *Times* report.[78] The *Times* published the announcement on March 28, and it was broadcast unaltered on the BBC Persian service the same day.[79] In Tehran, the ambassador, Sir Reader Bullard, voiced similar concerns regarding Iranian reaction to news of Reza Shah's illness. Seeking an immediate update on the ex-shah's health, he cabled, "Rumors of his death already circulating here." These rumors Bullard was instructed to deny.[80] Clifford was disappointed that the *Times*/BBC report did not also suggest that Reza Shah's medical problems predated his arrival in Mauritius and had originated in Iran, but Young at the FO dismissed the suggestion: "I think it would be difficult to verify in Tehran the story of the ex-Shah's previous illness," he wrote—and added, "We could hardly have taken the line the Governor suggests—the implications of it would have been too obvious."[81]

As it turned out, Reza Shah, attended by a team of three physicians in Mauritius, responded rapidly to treatment and by mid-April was well enough to leave. Better facilities were in any case were available in South Africa (e.g., the X-rays taken in Mauritius proved useless because of a faulty machine).

He boarded the SS *Empire Woodlark* on April 16, accompanied by his five sons, his personal secretary, two attendants, and H. D. Tonking, who was now assigned to continue serving as a medical and political adviser to Reza Shah. He arrived in Durban early in May.

The British had chosen Mauritius for Reza Shah's exile for the oft-stated reasons: they wanted to keep him far from his homeland, under British control, and where he could not become a target for Nazi intrigue or make trouble for them himself. They resisted his wish to transfer elsewhere in the British Empire because of the cost and the extensive arrangements such a move would entail in a time of war. They eventually relented due to pressure from Mohammad Reza Shah in Tehran and for fear that continued detention in Mauritius would lead to a breakdown in Reza Shah's morale and physical health. At the same time, they used Reza Shah's continued detention in Mauritius for leverage and the ex-shah himself as a "pawn" to speed up conclusion of the Tripartite Treaty, an agreement critical to the war effort.

Reza Shah was on the whole more content in South Africa, where he spent the last two years of his life, than he had been in Mauritius. He was still not a free man; he remained firmly in British hands. But he was at last free of his Mauritius "prison"—of the small, verdant island where he had begun his exile and which he had so intensely detested.

6

Johannesburg and the Death of Reza Shah

On arrival in Durban, Reza Shah found himself met, not by an official welcoming party, but by an ambulance. Forewarned by Clifford, the South African authorities had prepared the ambulance to take Reza Shah directly from Durban port to a nursing home. True to form, Reza Shah refused both ambulance and nursing home. He elected to go by automobile directly to the house British officials in South Africa had prepared for him. Reza Shah had always been loath to admit to personal frailty or a need for doctors and medicine. He was upset by inaccurate newspaper reports that on his arrival in Durban he was taken on a stretcher and by ambulance directly to a hospital.[1] In Mauritius, though feeling weak and unwell with stomach pain and hand tremors, he had rejected entreaties that a doctor should be called—until the heart attack made medical attention inevitable.[2] "I'm not one for taking medicine," he had told his private secretary, Ali Izadi. After the doctors arrived, he only reluctantly agreed to go to the hospital for X-rays. "Don't think for a minute that I am physically ill," he told Izadi. "I am in excellent health." His problem, he insisted, stemmed from the unease of mind he felt in exile and his concern about his country. All his life, he said, he had fled from ease and idleness: "A life not spent in the service of the nation is of no value," he remarked.[3] Now he had nothing to do.

In Durban, Tonking persuaded him only "with some difficulty" to submit to a full medical examination.[4] Reza Shah, however, "confounded the doctors by making a spectacular and rapid recovery,"[5] and by the time he arrived in Johannesburg a heart specialist, Walter May, found him much improved. May confirmed the ex-shah had experienced a cardiac breakdown and suffered some heart damage; but Reza Shah, he noted, was regaining weight, had cut down on smoking and alcohol consumption, and was looking healthy for his age: "His mind is obviously very active and his responses are quick," May noted. He encouraged Reza Shah to lead "a quiet and abstemious life" and to avoid "any severe exercise"—a reference to Reza Shah's penchant for taking long walks at least twice a day, a habit that for some reason May and other doctors, both British and local, considered "vigorous exercise" and inadvisable.[6] Commenting on the medical report at the Foreign Office (FO) in London, Young uncharitably observed, "There is no mention of opium smoking among the ex-Shah's 'social habits.' Perhaps supplies of 'tariak' [opium] have run out."[7]

Once in South Africa, Reza Shah decided he did not wish to risk the ocean voyage to Canada in a time of war or to go to Canada at all. Because he disliked living at sea level, he wished to move from Durban to Johannesburg. The South African prime minister, Jan Smuts, had initially agreed to allow Reza Shah and his party only to transit though South Africa on his way to Canada—then, when it was thought Reza Shah would arrive in South Africa a sick man requiring medical attention, to allow him to remain only as long as the "state of his health imperatively demands."[8] But Reza Shah put his foot down: if he were a free man, he should be able to travel where he wished; if he were not free, "then why was he paying his personal expenses?" He would go to Canada only "as a political prisoner," he said.[9] In the interests of the war effort and as a goodwill gesture to Britain, Smuts agreed that Reza Shah could reside in Johannesburg and be treated as a distinguished visitor. The FO expressed relief: "It is very helpful of the P.M. to allow the ex-Shah to reside in Johannesburg for the present," Pink at the FO noted. Moving Reza Shah to Canada entailed many difficulties, and dealing with him was not easy. "The Field Marshal may find that his distinguished guest is rather exacting and temperamental," he added.[10] As a result of this unanticipated sequence of events, Reza Shah spent the last two years of his life in exile in South Africa rather than in Canada.

Having allowed the ex-shah to remain, Smuts did not wish to see his new guest's relative calm upset in any way. In mid-June 1942, the governor of Mauritius requested the immediate return of Tonking; his services as a pathologist were required back on the island. Smuts forcefully intervened and asked Tonking be allowed to remain: "He feels very strongly that any action that might have the effect of disturbing the even tenor of the ex-Shah's way should be avoided," the high commissioner cabled to London. Smuts and his officials mustered the reasons and spelled out the many ways Tonking had become indispensable to the ex-shah and the royal family—and to the British. Reza Shah seemed reasonably happy in South Africa, and he and his sons were growing more favorably disposed toward Great Britain. "In view of the ex-Shah's influence over the present Shah and in Persia … continuance of this state of affairs is clearly desirable."[11] Tonking censored all the ex-shah's correspondence and supervised his accounts. He was successfully managing the royal children; and his able handling of the family had so far avoided untoward incidents. He had won the trust of Reza Shah who relied on him for advice on a range of matters.

The high commissioner concurred with Smuts, as did the Dominions Office (DO) and the FO. The Union government was asked to provide a pathologist to replace Tonking in Mauritius; and, as a result, Tonking remained with Reza Shah. During Reza Shah's two years in Johannesburg, Tonking became the principal interlocutor between the ex-shah and the South African and British authorities; and they came to rely on his assessments of Reza Shah's mood, mindset, and requirements. He dealt with the many problems of Reza Shah's sons. He was on hand when Reza Shah died, and he helped wind down his affairs after his death.

Johannesburg Days

Reza Shah and his family took the overnight train from Durban to Johannesburg. His cook, who had accompanied him from Mauritius, set up shop in a corner of the luggage car to cook his dinner. Until a house could be found and readied, the family stayed at the historic Langham Hotel. Reza Shah ate his meals in his room alone; the family ate in the hotel dining room.[12]

Reza Shah felt more comfortable in Johannesburg than he had felt in Mauritius—even if he did not remain content for long. The climate, with its pleasant summers and mild winters, suited him well and was closer to that of the Iranian uplands that he loved. In Mauritius, except for two occasions, he had refused to leave the compound where he was housed, insisting he was a prisoner and must behave like one. He took his daily walks in the garden of his Mauritius home. In Johannesburg (and during the brief stay in Durban), he ventured out often. In Durban he went with one of his sons, Mahmud Reza, to choose cutlery for the new household. Buying the cutlery did not prove simple. Reza Shah spoke no English; his son's English was severely limited. "It was difficult, quite a situation, to tell the store owner what one wanted and didn't want," Mahmud Reza later recalled.[13] On one occasion he suggested to his private secretary, Ali Izadi, that they walk the 10-kilometer distance from his house to the center of the city. Tired from the long walk, he agreed to a suggestion from Izadi and "for the first and last time" he sat down in a café and had a cup of tea.[14] In Johannesburg, he often took his walks in the city. On one of these walks, unaware that pedestrians had to observe traffic signals, he tried to cross against a red light on a busy street and was stopped and accosted by a policeman—an incident that greatly upset him. He enjoyed visiting the Johannesburg zoo, with its wild animals, and to walk along Zoo Lake with its famous musical fountain.[15] As always, he was attentive to everything he saw: in both Durban and Johannesburg and from the train window between the two cities. Reza Shah, at 65[16] and before his exile, had been out of Iran only twice. The first time, as prime minister in January 1925, he went on a brief pilgrimage to the Shi'ite shrine cities in Iraq; the second time, as shah in 1935, he visited Turkey as the guest of President Ataturk. He had not seen with his own eyes a modern, industrialized European country—the kind of country that he had hoped and strived for Iran to become. Now, he was struck to see what he understood to be European-style cities in Africa. In both Durban and Johannesburg, he was impressed with the multistory buildings, the broad avenues, the cleanliness of the city streets, and the orderliness of the people getting on and off trains and going about their business. He was particularly struck by the large presence of women in public spaces, "wearing men's clothes" and driving taxis and even trucks. He was surprised to learn that the grocer and the washerwoman who arrived at the house were driving their own automobiles.[17]

In Johannesburg, the isolation Reza Shah had felt in Mauritius was relieved by his ability to receive visitors from Iran. In June 1942, Ernest Perron, a confidante of the ruling shah, arrived with a message from son to father and to settle some family business. Perron brought a gramophone record with greetings from Mohammad Reza Shah to his father. He was followed by Manuchehr Moqaddam who was to serve as the new private secretary. (Izadi wished to return home; but it was in the end Izadi who remained and Moqaddam who left early). In April 1943, Princess Ashraf, Reza Shah's second eldest daughter and the twin sister of the ruling shah, came to spend six weeks with her father. Reza Shah, always hungry for news about the situation in Iran, eagerly read the letters from family members and the newspapers and magazines all three brought with them. When Princess Ashraf arrived, he almost immediately bombarded her with questions about Iran and about his son.[18] He continued in Johannesburg the ritual he had begun in Mauritius, of listening every evening to the Persian news broadcasts of the BBC and Radio Berlin and, when it could be successfully accessed, the news on Radio Tehran.

Tonking dutifully reported to the DO on his conversations with both Perron and Moqaddam; but, court gossip and random opinions aside, he does not appear to have gleaned much useful intelligence for British officials. Perron was of the opinion that the current shah's policy of close collaboration with England would not have been possible had Reza Shah remained in power; the return of Reza Shah to Iran would spell the end of Anglo-Iranian cooperation, he said. Moqaddam, on the other hand, took the view that the return to Iran of Reza Shah was essential to control rebellious and pro-German elements, as the young shah lacked the requisite ruthlessness to do so. Both men spoke of the effectiveness of pro-Axis propaganda in Iran. Perron, who sought to depict himself as thoroughly pro-British, suggested he had to hurry back to prevent court intrigue from undermining him and his pro-British influence. Moqaddam worried about the food situation at home and predicted widespread famine should German advances push Soviet troops based in the Caucasus into Iran.[19]

A "Dark-Skinned Family": Color Bar Problems

When Reza Shah decided to take up residence in Johannesburg, British officials feared that the South African color bar would prove problematic or lead to embarrassing moments. As Young at the FO noted, "The ex-Shah's party are bound to have uncomfortable moments. Unfortunately, they are a rather dark-skinned family."[20] Tonking, too, observed that difficulties are always likely to arise while the party are in the Union of South Africa and move about freely ... Of the party the Crown Prince [Ali Reza] is definitely the most Asiatic in appearance, the others not being anything like as dark ... The whole situation is further complicated in that they look on themselves as being completely and wholly white.[21]

Tonking took the precaution of notifying places of public entertainment of the advent of the princes and suggested to the Department of External Affairs that they provide members of the royal family with identity cards.

As it turned out, these fears were not born out. No incidents involving members of the royal family and the color bar were reported to London by British officials in the Union; in interviews conducted many years later, members of the family did not recall unpleasant color bar-related experiences during their South African stay. The older boys seemed to have encountered no problems in enjoying what entertainment Johannesburg had to offer or engaging in what Tonking described as their "amorous adventures." The South African government had in any case downplayed the presence of the Iranian royal family in South Africa. No officials were on hand to receive Reza Shah when he landed in Durban or when he relocated to Johannesburg. According to Izadi, "We entered Johannesburg like ordinary travelers and made our home at the Langham hotel unrecognized and unknown." The major newspapers made only passing reference to the ex-shah's arrival and the family's doings in Johannesburg.[22] No Union official was apparently assigned to Reza Shah: "No one was charged with supervising what he did ... for example in taking walks or shopping. He did what he wanted to do," his son, Mahmud Reza, recalled.[23]

In September 1942, the editor of the weekly newspaper, *Forward*, did splash a long article on its front and inside pages that Reza Shah was living a life of luxury in Johannesburg, despite—the newspaper claimed—his notorious pro-Nazi sympathies and the demand of the Iranian government he be repatriated to face trial in Iran. The editor, in a cable, offered the London newspaper, the *Herald*, an "outstanding story" along the same lines. There was no press censorship in South Africa, and the publication of such stories could not be prevented; but cables could be censored and the censor blocked the editor's telegram and offer to the *Herald*.[24] London was relieved. "The less publicity given to the ex-Shah, the better," minuted Young at the FO.[25]

The high commissioner and the South African authorities suspected the Soviet consulate of instigating the article, which alleged the ex-shah would have been treated differently (by implication, less kindly) had he been sent to Russia.[26] British officials explained to the Iranians that the *Forward*, the organ of the Left Party, was an unimportant newspaper with only a small circulation; London newspapers did not pick up the story; and while the report left Reza Shah unhappy, it proved to be a passing incident.

The color problem did arise for British and South African officials in the search for a new house for Reza Shah in early 1943. Reza Shah disliked the two houses rented for him in Johannesburg. The landlord did not complete on time repairs, which he had undertaken to carry out and for which Reza Shah had paid him £500.[27] The rent was high. The landlord was charging £50 a month for residences the rent board assessed at only £33.[28] The houses were small for such a large family. Perron, during his visit in June 1942, was surprised to see the royal family so poorly housed and suggested that funds might be sent from Tehran to purchase a house for Reza Shah. British officials agreed that the current residence was unsuitable. Reza Shah complained of the small size of his bedroom and told Tonking that the British government "are completely indifferent to the circumstances in which he has to live." Tonking, believing that Reza Shah would remain "quiet and contented" in South Africa if the housing problem were resolved,[29] in January 1943 picked up on Perron's suggestion and began in earnest a search for a house that Reza Shah could buy.

Immediately, color bar concerns emerged, resulting in a flurry of exchanges between Tonking, the British high commissioner's office in Pretoria, the South African authorities, and London.[30] South African statutes, such as the Gold Law, barred purchase or occupation by "Asiatics" of property in "reserved areas." These reserved areas included Johannesburg and large parts of the Transvaal. Reza Shah, however, insisted on being in Johannesburg or near the center of the city; he refused to consider areas further away and exempt from the statutory restrictions against colored occupation. "To obviate difficulties arising from the legal disabilities of Asiatics," Tonking proposed as a solution that the house be purchased in the name of the British government.[31] But this subterfuge—a violation of South African law—was rejected in London as inadvisable. South African officials, in turn, rejected as unfeasible, and bound to lead to questions in Parliament, a suggestion by an FO official that the Union government act as householder for the ex-shah.[32] Tonking reported in early March his search was proving fruitless. He had placed ads in two newspapers and had numerous agents looking, but the anti-Asiatic clauses ruled out practically all the suitable housing in the Transvaal and elsewhere. Reza Shah might have to continue to rent, concluded Ben Cockburn, the political secretary to the high commissioner.[33] "I think ... [Tonking] is sick to death of looking for houses," commented another official in the high commissioner's office.[34]

Tonking was able to renew the lease on one of the two houses occupied by the royal family for another two months at a higher price.[35] He now looked for a house to rent. In March he cabled that the "housing problem [was] resolving itself"; and in April he reported that Reza Shah had signed a twelve-month lease on a spacious house, large enough for the entire party, with five acres in a walled garden on 41 Young Avenue, Mountain View, a good district of Johannesburg, not subject to the Gold Law.[36] This was not the end of concern over the color problem, however. The title deeds to the Young Avenue house, as was common in Johannesburg, prohibited leases to "Coolies, Asiatics or Coloured Persons" and allowed any householder in the district to obtain an eviction order from a magistrate. Tonking worried that a situation might arise requiring him to tell Reza Shah that "he and his family rank as Asiatics, and that he would have to leave the house at once." He urged that the Union government be asked to ensure that the racial clauses should be "rendered inoperative" or to grant the royal family diplomatic immunity;[37] but he was informed the color bar would apply equally to diplomats, whether the high commissioner for India or an ex-Japanese minister.[38] The high commissioner's office even considered asking the Union government to request that the local magistrate not issue an eviction order—but this idea went nowhere are well.[39] "There is now a lot of potential trouble ahead ... The ex-Shah will ... continually have the sword of Damocles hanging over his head," a Union official noted, since any owner of a property in the township or municipality could demand eviction; and the South African department of interior had no power to cancel the discrimination clauses in the title deeds. "We can only hope that you can keep the party straight so that they do not trouble the neighbors and that the neighbors themselves do not create trouble." Much depended on the behavior of the members of Reza Shah's household, "particularly the sons with their high-powered cars," a Union official added.[40] The behavior of Reza Shah's five sons, particularly the two older boys, was a persistent source of concern to Tonking and the South African authorities. The boys had several cars at their disposal, and their consumption of gasoline was high at a time of gas rationing for other South Africans. The South African authorities disapproved of the "gay time" they were having in and around Johannesburg in a time of war,[41] and other officials expressed alarm that the royal entourage was using seven motor cars, fearing a "public scandal" due to the petrol consumption of the princes.[42]

A Burning Issue: Educating the Princes

Reza Shah's five sons were also not getting a proper education. (The two youngest children, Princess Fatemeh and Hamid, aged 14 and 10, had returned to Iran when Reza Shah left Mauritius for Durban.) The three oldest boys, at around 18, 19, and 20 when in Johannesburg, were already beyond school age. The boys had tutors while in Mauritius. In Johannesburg, the tutoring was spotty. The attempts—mostly to no avail—to arrange for a proper education for the boys involved, in time, officials in Johannesburg, London, and the royal court in Tehran; the Iranian and British ambassadors in Cairo; and even the educational director of the British Council. These efforts present a kind of mirror to the loss of moorings, the dislocations, caused to the royal family by exile. During his June 1942 visit, Perron was unhappy to see that the boys' only amusements were cinemas and cabarets and that they were neglecting their education. Tonking later observed that it was difficult in South Africa to find a suitable person who spoke French fluently and English "without a colonial accent," but he did manage to engage a Miss Bretagne, "a middle-aged gentlewoman," to give the boys English lessons.[43] This did not prove adequate for the education of the boys.

In Tehran, Mohammad Reza Shah, distressed to hear from Perron that his brothers were leading a life of "complete idleness," decided they needed a first-class tutor and proposed sending to Johannesburg a Swiss schoolmaster, Alfred Beauverd, who had been his teacher at the Le Rosey School in Rolle, Switzerland, and whom he highly respected.[44] The British consul in Berne, instructed to make enquiries, reported home that Beauverd was in every way "politically unexceptionable." This cleared the way for a British green light, and the Union authorities agreed to grant Beauverd a visa. Reza Shah, however, who in general avoided foreigners, vetoed the proposal.[45]

By July 1943, the royal family had already been in Johannesburg for a full year, yet the problem of the boys' education remained unresolved. Tonking explained that the two younger boys, aged 16 and 17, could not attend the local schools: their level education was low; they lacked the necessary language skills and would have to attend classes with much younger boys; and the color barrier posed an additional obstacle. He also felt they should be removed from the influence of their older brothers "who are liable to get them into scrapes."[46] Reza Shah preferred to send the two boys back to Iran to complete their education; but Bullard, the ambassador in Tehran, thought this a bad idea and reported that the ruling shah agreed: The boys would not complete their education; they would idle away their time and get into bad habits.[47]

Compounding the problem of arranging for the education of the princes was the very low opinion British officials entertained of the boys' educational level and abilities—opinions they did not wish publicized. According to Tonking, the older princes were "not educated to a standard comparable with our Lower Certificate Examination ... they never had the stimulus of competitive study."[48] Later in the process, B. P. Sullivan, the acting high commissioner in Pretoria, sharing cables from the Dominions Office about the young princes' schooling and educational level, instructed Tonking "to read and destroy [them] by fire." Two weeks later, he shared with Tonking another cable on the same subject from the DO and asked him to "burn ... as soon as you read and digested it."[49]

Mohammad Reza Shah decided to send his brothers to Beirut, or preferably to the elite British school, Victoria College, in Alexandria (a school Bullard also suggested). The headmaster of Victoria College, R. W. G. Reed, approached by the Iranian ambassador, did not relish the prospect of admitting the boys, whom he considered too old for entry, but he said he would acquiesce if necessary. The British ambassador, Lord Killearn, however, did not believe it in Britain's interest to have the boys in Egypt and advised against it. They would be exposed to the anti-British sentiments of the palace, he wrote. He also advised against sending the boys to Beirut where the boys would be subject to French or American, rather than British, influence. He recommended, instead, that the princes be sent to England. The court minister, Hussein Ala, recommended England as well; but Bullard thought there was little chance of finding a tutor in wartime.[50]

With Egypt and Beirut ruled out, and England uncertain, Ahmad and Mahmud returned to Iran in October 1943. Later that year or in early 1944, Mohammad Reza shah decided it essential that his four youngest siblings, Ahmad Reza, Mahmud Reza, Hamid Reza, and Fatemeh, go at once to Beirut or Cairo to continue their education. Both he and Reza Shah felt that remaining in Tehran would be harmful to their characters.[51] In Egypt, Lord Killearn once again strongly objected: "I still think it not in our interest the Princes should be educated in Egypt or Beirut and that it would be better for them to be sent to England."[52] The FO next picked up on the suggestion by Killearn and also by Bullard and court minister Ala that the boys be sent to England. C. W. Baxter, the head of the eastern department at the FO, consulted Ifor Evans, the educational director of the British Council, about finding a suitable tutor for the boys in England.[53] Before this avenue could be further pursued, however, the shah arranged for all three younger boys to attend the American college in Beirut and made separate arrangements for Princess Fatemeh, who accompanied them.

Keeping Watch

There was a flip side to Reza Shah's and the ruling shah's belief that returning to Tehran exposed the younger siblings to undesirable influences. British officials also opposed the return to Iran of the older brothers, believing their behavior would damage the standing of the royal court and harm the shah. Yet the princes were growing restless and wanted to return home. Gholam Reza cabled his brother, the shah, directly requesting permission to do so; the eldest, Ali Reza, pressed to return "to take his rightful role as Crown Prince."[54]

Bullard had already suggested that it was undesirable for the shah to have any more of his relatives around him; he thought it especially undesirable for the eldest, Ali Reza, who was "likely to have an especially bad influence in court circles," to return to Iran.[55] Informed in late 1943 that Ali Reza asked to come home, Bullard's response was uncompromisingly negative. He reported that he went to see court minister Ala, who was "horrified" at the idea that Ali Reza should return, and added, "He knows even more than we do about the unpleasant escapades in which Ali Reza was mixed up during the last year or two he was in Persia, and he said no girl was safe from Ali Reza." Bullard found the shah also unenthusiastic and "taken aback" that his brother wished to come home. "The return of Ali Reza would be a disaster for the Shah," Bullard added. "It would provide an excellent pretext for any general who wished to turn out the Pahlavis and take their place."[56] The boys were told the moment was not opportune for their return and remained in Johannesburg until after Reza Shah's death.

Although members of the royal family were much freer in Johannesburg than in Mauritius, British oversight remained in place. Letters from family members in Johannesburg were checked by Tonking and often also the high commissioner's office in Pretoria and the censor's office in Cairo before being sent on to Tehran.[57] Travel outside Johannesburg was subject to South African approval; and British approval was required for any family member to return to Iran, or for a relative from Iran to visit Johannesburg. The application of these restrictions was common. In 1943, the foreign secretary, Anthony Eden, directed that Reza Shah should not be allowed to receive any further visits from his relatives.[58] The Union authorities disapproved when the two older boys wanted to spend Christmas at a hotel in Durban. Tonking had to secure permission, through the high commissioner's office, for Prince Gholam Reza to take a month's holiday on the south coast. The Swiss tutor, Beauverd, as noted, required both South African and British concurrence to come to Johannesburg. When Bullard was approached with a proposal that Reza Shah be joined by his wife, he was instructed by Johannesburg "to give the Persian court no encouragement to expect that travel facilities will be granted until authorities here have had time to consider matter further."[59] The FO was not pleased when it learned that, at the request of the British embassy in Tehran, the South African authorities gave Princess Shams, Reza Shah's oldest daughter, permission to visit her father. "Tehran should have consulted us before applying for a passage for Princess Shams," minuted Young at the FO.[60] By then, Reza Shah was gravely ill, and the FO decided on compassionate grounds to allow her visit.

A Place Nearer Home?

Reza Shah himself had been growing increasingly reclusive. His private secretary noted that he avoided people, had grown attuned to being alone, and rarely ventured down from his room before noon. He always ate his meals in his room alone. The advent of Now Ruz, the Iranian New Year, which coincides with the spring equinox and which Iranian families traditionally celebrated together as a moment of rebirth, hope, and new beginnings, Izadi recalled, was always the worst time of the year for the ex-shah. Marking Now Ruz with the family in March 1944, Reza Shah seemed to Izadi more crestfallen than usual.[61] To his daughter Shams in Tehran, he wrote, "My physical condition is not bad; but as to my state of mind, it is better not to speak."[62] Repeatedly, he told Tonking that the weather in Johannesburg did not suit him; that he wished to transfer to a country under British control but nearer Iran, where family members could more easily visit him. (His reputation as a stern and even fearsome ruler notwithstanding, Reza Shah was attached to his family; the need for family members to remain united and treat one another well is a persistent theme in his letters to his son, daughters, and wife in Iran.)[63] In July 1943, Tonking reported, he urgently reiterated this request.[64]

British officials in London were unmoved. Were H. M. G. to yield to Reza Shah's every whim to move, he would not settle anywhere, the DO replied to Tonking. Moving him nearer Iran was inadvisable, creating the impression the British were preparing to return him to Persia, and this would have a disturbing political effect. Tonking should remind the ex-shah that he himself had chosen to live in South Africa; His Majesty's Government had gone to great lengths to see him well taken care of; a war was on and it was difficult to arrange for family members to visit him. In brief, H. M. G. could not move him at this time.[65] Pressed by Reza Shah, Tonking returned to the subject of relocating Reza Shah in November 1943. He reported to the DO that while Reza Shah had been well since his arrival in Johannesburg and the heart problems he experienced in Durban had not recurred, "he is an old man … The possibility of his death at any time should be borne in mind." Britain should prepare for such an eventuality, he wrote, and make plans for securing private papers, the disposal and perhaps the embalming of the remains, payment of outstanding debts, and provisions for the other members of the family.[66] Could he at least tell Reza Shah that, after the war, he could live in any country of his choosing and that would accept him?

At the FO, Baxter decried the idea; and in Tehran, Bullard agreed: Tonking was worrying prematurely; and it was "out of the question" to raise the matter of Reza Shah's declining health with the ruling shah, until there were more definite signs his father was seriously ill.[67] Britain should not commit itself to allowing Reza Shah to live in a country of own choosing after war, Bullard cabled. "As you know, we are anxious that he should remain as far away as possible from Persia, and his presence in a neighboring country might not at the end of the war be to our interests or those of Persia and the present Shah." Britain might find itself in the uncomfortable position of pressuring Reza Shah to reside in a country further from Persia than he would wish; so went Bullard's reasoning.

The FO, in fact, concluded that "it would not be advisable or practicable to compel the ex-Shah indefinitely to remain in a country where he did not want to live," but nevertheless agreed that no commitment should be made to Reza Shah at present that he could live in a country of his own choosing after the war. This decision was conveyed via the DO to the high commissioner and to Tonking.[68] Tonking merely told Reza Shah that South Africa was the best country in the world for him at present and the question of his place of residence could be reconsidered when the war is over.[69]

In March 1944, the high commissioner in South Africa sent a more urgent cable to the DO. Reza Shah had again spoken to Tonking about leaving South Africa.

> Tonking says that, contrary to his usual custom, the ex-Shah returned again and again to this subject during a two hour interview, and ascribes this insistence to a desire to be nearer home in the event of his death … [Tonking] reports that he has heard from the secretary to the ex-Shah that he told his sons he hoped this would be the last year of his life. Tonking has observed that the ex-Shah has aged in the last year.[70]

But the FO refused to budge. "I do not see what modification we can make in our … feelings about this," observed one FO official; and Young so informed the DO. "I am afraid there is nothing for it but to maintain the line we have already taken and to give the ex-Shah no encouragement whatever to expect that he will be moved. If we show any sign of weakening in face of his importunity, it will only be redoubled."[71]

Tonking was instructed to inform Reza Shah that he must stay in Johannesburg for the present and did so: "He took it well," Tonking reported to the high commissioner, "but said that as soon as the war in Europe was over he was leaving, even if on foot. I told him I should be delighted to walk with him."[72]

Reza Shah experienced his fatal heart attack two months later.

"His Majesty Won't Wake Up"

By June 1944 Reza Shah's physical condition had visibly deteriorated, and he had grown much weaker. He complained that he felt unwell but, as usual, he refused medication, insisting that he suffered from nothing more than indigestion. He was now taking his daily walk in his own bedroom; and his private secretary, Izadi, noticed one morning that he could barely manage even this brief pacing.[73] The heart attack occurred well before dawn on the morning of June 25, as Reza Shah was making his way to the bathroom. He managed to stumble back to his bed, falling and suffering cuts on his hand and face. Summoned to his bedside at 5:30 a.m., Tonking and an attending physician, Dr. Brossy, found Reza Shah "gravely collapsed" with a barely perceptible heart rate and severe breathing difficulties. His skin had a bluish hue, a sign of deep cyanosis. Tonking and Brossy thought recovery after such a severe attack impossible, but Reza Shah rallied after injections of Coramine and the administration of oxygen. A week later, he was again experiencing severe respiratory distress; and other doctors and a heart specialist were called in.[74]

Tonking now anticipated at least a short-term recovery; and, to Izadi too, Reza Shah seemed better. He could get up from bed and walk around his room. He even ventured into the garden. The arrival of his daughter, Princess Shams, boosted his spirits. On the evening of July 25, with Shams there, he chatted and engaged in the banter he sometimes used with his staff.

But the recovery proved brief. Early on the morning of July 26, Izadi was awakened by loud knocking on his bedroom door. It was Reza Shah's personal servant, Mahmud. "His Majesty won't wake up," Mahmud said. Izadi dressed and hurried to Reza Shah's side. He appeared to Izadi to be sleeping. "The look on his face was peaceful. There was no sign of death on it." His hand was still warm to Izadi's touch. "How is your Excellency's health?" Izadi asked. His master did not respond.[75] Reza Shah had passed away. His long, unhappy exile had ended.

7

Wrapping Up

There was left only the business of wrapping up the loose ends: arranging for the final resting place for Reza Shah's remains; determining where Reza Shah's sons would go after South Africa; securing Reza Shah's papers and belongings and dealing with his estate; and, for Britain, issuing a proper condolence message to the ruling shah in Iran.

Tonking's advice to his superiors seven months earlier that they must prepare for Reza Shah's death and for dealing with precisely such matters had been treated as premature and unnecessarily alarmist by both the Foreign Office and the British ambassador in Tehran. Tonking had nevertheless taken the precaution of alerting undertakers to prepare for the embalming of the body. He had also asked the law firm, Moodie and Robertson, which had done some minor legal work for Reza Shah, to take over the handling of the estate.

Once he had confirmed Reza Shah had passed away, Tonking invited members of the family to take a last look at the body (Princess Shams and Princes Ali Reza did so, the two younger sons did not). In the presence of the private secretary, Ali Izadi, Tonking then collected all Reza Shah's papers and valuables and locked and sealed them in a closet. He locked the suite and took the keys with him. He returned five days later with Izadi, a representative of the Robertson law firm, and a sworn appraiser to draw up an inventory of the ex-shah's papers and belongings and to evaluate virtually everything: valuables, carpets, furniture, dress uniforms, and the like.[1] Tonking also took a dress uniform, military decorations, and a dress sword to the undertakers to prepare for the "lying in state." In keeping with Iranian tradition, the informal lying in state took place seven days after Reza Shah's death and was attended by members of the family and personal staff.[2]

Grudging Condolences; Grudging Farewell

It is a measure of the lingering rancor toward Reza Shah among British officials that the simple business of expressing official condolences to Mohammad Reza Shah, the ruling monarch and Reza Shah's eldest son, proved problematical. Initially, officials dealing with Iran at the FO concluded that a simple message from King George VI to Mohammad Reza Shah would be adequate. As W. H. Young at the FO explained, "The intention is only to convey a private message of sympathy to the Shah on his father's death, not to send any formal message regretting the demise of the ex-Shah." Sir Reader Bullard, back in England on home leave, concurred.[3] Sir Maurice Peterson, now the head of the eastern and far eastern departments at the FO, wrote in this vein to Sir Alan Lascelles, private secretary to King George: "In view of the circumstances in which he [Reza Shah] left Persia, we do not think any formal message from The King would be appropriate. At the same time, the Shah will almost certainly take it amiss if he receives no message of condolence." The FO proposed that the British ambassador in Tehran inform the court minister that the king "has been grieved" to learn of the loss the shah had suffered and expressed his sympathies. Lascelles telephoned from Buckingham palace that the king had agreed.[4]

But only three days later, Peterson wrote to the king's private secretary again to apologize and to say the FO was withdrawing the suggestion. The foreign secretary, Anthony Eden, had not been consulted, Peterson wrote, and "has now said he would rather no message were sent to the Shah. We are taking no action."[5] Daniel Lascelles, the British embassy counselor in Tehran and in charge during Bullard's absence, urged reconsideration. The shah, he reported, seemed a good deal hurt by the absence of any message of condolence from the king. Eden now changed his mind and decided that royal condolences were appropriate; Buckingham Palace was so informed; and a message of sympathy from King George to the shah was finally conveyed through the embassy in Tehran.

Arranging for Reza Shah's remains to be sent to Iran also led to an extended correspondence that mirrors the disconnect between official British and official Iranian views of Reza Shah's place in Iranian history. For the British, the remains of Reza Shah had of course to be treated with respect; but the return home of the ex-shah's remains was simply a matter of identifying the most practical means of doing so. For the ruling shah in Iran, Reza Shah was a towering figure in the modern history of his country; the return of his remains to his homeland had to be so arranged so as to pay him the homage he deserved. Reza Shah's body had been immediately embalmed, but in the three months that followed, various options were proposed and considered by the Court in Tehran and the FO and then rejected by one side or the other: to ship the body by air or by sea; if by sea on what kind of a vessel and to what port: to an Iranian Persian Gulf port, to Basra in Iraq, to Bombay in India, or to Suez in Egypt? And would the arrival of the remains on Iranian soil be simply an "arrival" or an occasion for solemn ceremonies?

The Court in Tehran initially asked for the embalmed body to be shipped to the Persian Gulf port of Basra, preferably on a warship, in order to show due respect to Reza Shah, from where it could be easily transported back to Iranian soil. But the request for warship transport was quickly squashed: "the idea of laying on a warship is absurd," minuted an FO official.[6] The FO informed the Tehran embassy that except for oil tankers there were virtually no direct sailings from South Africa to the Persian Gulf and that "there can of course be no question of laying on a warship."[7] Lacelles, in Tehran, cabled back that he had sounded out Iranian officials, and the Court was "clearly horrified" at the idea of using a tanker. If no warship were available, he suggested shipping the remains directly to an Iranian port, Khorramshahr or Bandar Shapour, so that the Persians could arrange the last stage of the journey to Tehran, by rail, "with sufficient pomp." He added, "This is the sort of matter on which the Shah feels strongly and, and in regard to which we consequently stand to gain or lose a great deal in terms of political good will." War conditions notwithstanding, he urged reconsideration.[8]

The FO was not persuaded. It suggested shipment of the remains to Bombay (sailings from South Africa to Bombay were frequent) then transfer to another vessel headed for an Iranian port.[9] But the Iranians rejected the Bombay route due to the length of time required and because the body would arrive in Iran without sufficient pomp. They suggested the body be flown directly to Tehran; but the British felt they could not provide aircraft for the purpose in a time of war. Lascelles cabled home that he had "embroidered considerably" on the difficulty of providing air passage but that the Iranians remained unhappy.

When the American police adviser, Stephen Timmerman, was killed in a riot in 1944, they pointed out, the US bomber authorities provided direct air transport home. Lascelles again appealed: "The Shah is greatly influenced politically by such considerations and our political interests are correspondingly affected. I much hope your decision can be reconsidered in this light"—but to no avail.[10]

The Iranians now reverted to an earlier British proposal that the remains should be sent to Egypt; they would assume responsibility for the final journey to Iran. Even this suggestion proved problematical. Lascelles had earlier reported that Iran lacked the pilots capable of transporting the body to Iran on an Iranian aircraft. Now he warned that if the remains were sent by sea to Egypt, the Iranians would expect the body to be flown to Iran on British aircraft and with a British escort.[11]But Eden remained adamant:

> I am not prepared to press for air transport from South Africa (and) I would much prefer we not be associated with the actual delivery of the body to Persia. If we arranged sufficient display to satisfy Persian Court there might well be criticism here and in Persia. If we did not, Court would be offended.

If left with no other choices, Eden added, he would agree to provide British aircraft for the last stage of the journey and only if locally arranged, "but in no circumstances will British escort be provided."[12]

Six weeks later, Bullard put in a final plea: "I hope you will agree to conveyance of the body of the late Shah by [the British airline] B. O. A. C. as far as Basra. All other courses are beset with considerable difficulties." The body could then be carried by lorry, or truck, to Khorramshahr and then by train to Tehran, he said; and addressing the FO's reluctance to be associated in any way with honoring Reza Shah, Bullard made sure to add: "British authorities should however have nothing to do with the matter once the body has left the aircraft not even by lending transport, let alone taking part in ceremony."[13] The FO still refused air transport and the Iranian Court, having exhausted all other options, acceded to sea passage.[14]

In late October 1944, Reza Shah's body was finally transported from South Africa by ship to the Egyptian port of Suez and then by a special train to Cairo. If the British had grudged Reza any formal display of esteem, the Egyptian authorities did him full honors. (With good reason. There was a family connection: King Farouk's sister, Fawzia, was married to the ruling shah in

Iran.) Egyptian dignitaries were present when the late shah's remains arrived at Suez. At the Cairo train station, on hand to greet the arrival of the train carrying Reza Shah's remains were King Farouq's grand chamberlain, members of the royal family, the prime minister and members of his cabinet, Egyptian notables, and members of the diplomatic corps. An honor guard of royal marines laid the body, draped with the Iranian flag, on the a cannon bed. As the entourage left for the Mosque of al-Kakhia, salvos were fired and aircraft of the royal air force flew overhead. An army band played Chopin's funeral march—an honor that, given his disdain for the aping of things foreign, must have elicited a wry smile from the spirit of Reza Shah, had it been stirring. After prayers at the al-Kakhia Mosque, the body was finally laid to rest in the royal mausoleum in the al-Rifa'i Mosque. It remained there until 1950 when Reza Shah's remains were finally returned to Iranian soil.

Reporting on these events by relying on a report in the Cairo newspaper, *Journal d'Egypte*, Lord Killearn, the British ambassador in Cairo, hastened to add: "No British representative was present at [the Suez ceremony] or other ceremony."[15]

"A Relief to Hear the Last of Them"

Princess Shams had returned to Iran shortly after the death of her father. Her younger brothers, aged 18, 19, and 20, did not immediately follow. Ambassador Bullard, as already noted, had already suggested it undesirable for the shah to have any more of his relatives around him, and Mohammad Reza Shah himself preferred keeping his brothers away from the royal court. Pending a decision, the FO asked the Union authorities to allow the boys to remain in South Africa for the time being, although Tonking had thought they would not agree: "The reputation established by these young men may well make the Union authorities reluctant to accede to such a request now that the last shreds of parental control have been broken."[16]

Mohammad Reza Shah, in fact, had grander aspirations for his younger brothers. At the end of August, the Iranian ambassador to Cairo, just back from Tehran, conveyed three requests from his monarch to the British ambassador: that the eldest of the brothers, Ali Reza, be attached as an aide-de-camp to some British general (he suggested either General Henry Maitland Wilson or General Harold Alexander. Both men had served as commanders of British forces in the Middle East); that his two younger brothers be placed in military academies in Britain (e.g., Sandhurst) or in the United States (e.g., West Point); and that the boys should be allowed to come to Egypt pending these arrangements. A similar request was put to the American ambassador.[17] Lord Killearn, had objected to an earlier proposal that the royal princes attend school in Egypt, and his position remained obdurate: "I still strongly dislike prospect of these three Princes being in Egypt for any length of time," he wrote.[18] As it turned out the princes did not attend these prestigious military academies. To the relief of British officials, the boys, along with the private secretary, accompanied the body of their father from South Africa to Egypt: "We were relieved to hear the last of the ex-Shah and his family," a British official commented on hearing of their departure.[19] After Reza Shah's funeral in Egypt, the boys were sent to schools and colleges in the United States to complete their education.

Home at Last?

Reza Shah's remains finally came home six years later. His son, Mohammad Reza, waited—for the end of the Second World War, for things at home to settle down, and until he could prepare a homecoming befitting his late father. He ordered the erection of an imposing mausoleum to Reza Shah outside the capital, in Shahr-e Ray, a shrine city. When construction was completed in May 1950, Reza Shah's remains were transported via Jedda, Saudi Arabia, to the Iranian city of Ahwaz, then carried by special train to the capital. Ceremonial stops were arranged in towns along the route, including at the religious city of Qum, where there took place the traditional circumambulation of the body around the shrine of Ma'sumeh, a revered sister of the Shi'ite Imam Reza. In recognition of Reza Shah's military standing—he always regarded himself, above all, a soldier and military man—foreign governments were invited to send military representatives to the ceremonies and several countries did so. The coffin, mounted on a cannon and accompanied by Mohammad Reza Shah, his brothers, other members of the royal family, the prime minister and cabinet officers, members of the two houses of the Parliament, and foreign ambassadors, was carried to Shahr-e Ray and interred in a crypt in the mausoleum.[20]

There the mausoleum stood for a quarter of a century. Foreign dignitaries and heads of state on official visits to Iran paid their respects to Reza Shah by laying a wreath at his tomb. Ceremonies in 1975 marking the fiftieth anniversary of the establishment of the Pahlavi dynasty took place at the mausoleum site. Yet in history's unpredictable twists and turns, the mausoleum did not stand for long. The men who overthrew the Pahlavi dynasty and established the Islamic Republic in 1979, and who imagined they were recreating the ideal community established by the Prophet in the seventh-century Arabia, harbored a special venom for the architect of modern Iran. One of their first acts was to take pickax and shovel, bulldozer and wrecking ball, to destroy Reza Shah's mausoleum. Where there had stood a majestic structure meant to remind generations to come of Reza Shah's greatness, there remained only rubble—unsightly piles of shattered marble, brick, and once-laudatory inscriptions. For the new masters of Iran, the ruins represented an erasure, as it were, of over half a century of Pahlavi rule and the dawn of a new, Islamic era. Yet only four decades after this act of erasure, protestors on Tehran's streets, angry at a revolution whose promises had failed them and nostalgic for Reza Shah, or what they imagined Reza Shah had been, were evoking Reza Shah as an implicit rebuke to Iran's new rulers—among their slogans: "Reza Shah, may God rest your soul in peace." For Iran's new rulers, the "return" of Reza Shah must have seemed like a bad dream. They imagined they had relegated Reza Shah and all he represented to the dustbin of history. Now he confronted them again, not in real life but as a legend, as a reminder of what Iran had once achieved. Reza Shah was long gone; but his countrymen were still grappling with and quarreling over the meaning of his legacy.

8

"Where Do I Go without Money?" Reza Shah's Finances in Exile

It remains for us to consider Reza Shah's finances in exile and the contentious, drawn-out dispute over the settlement of his estate.

When Reza Shah died in exile in Johannesburg, South Africa, in July 1944, he left in his account at Barclays Bank a deposit of £110,000. This was a considerable sum of money at the time, equivalent in 2015 purchasing power to £4 million or $11 million.[1] Yet when he went into exile only three years earlier, Reza Shah feared he would be hard-pressed for money, if not left altogether destitute—and with some reason. Having abdicated his throne, Reza Shah had also transferred to his son and successor, Mohammad Reza Pahlavi, all his enormous wealth in properties, agricultural land, hotels, and factories, including 683 million rials in bank deposits. The cash in his bank account alone translated into £9.8 million at the 1941 exchange rate.[2] The new shah was to use these resources for schools, hospitals, and the general public welfare, but the transfer meant Reza Shah was left with no money of his own. As noted in Chapter 4, he was going into exile with a party of nineteen others: his third wife, Esmat, her step-sister and a lady-in-waiting, six sons and two daughters, his private secretary, his son-in-law, who served as his aide, a cook, and five additional servants.

"I haven't a penny to my name ... where am I to go with horde," he asked, referring to his numerous progeny?[3] About to leave his home for exile abroad he wanted to be certain he would have adequate funds in his new life; and he waited for confirmation that his son had arranged for the transfer of foreign exchange to cover his expenses abroad. As he made his way across Iran, with brief stays in Isfahan, Yazd, and Kerman, heading for the port of Bandar Abbas and exile, the problem of money was much on his mind. In Kerman, he inquired if foreign exchange could be purchased from local banks.[4] From his court minister, who accompanied him until he boarded ship at Bandar Abbas, he asked how much money remained in the foreign bank account set up to pay for the crown prince's education at a Swiss boarding school. (The amount left in the account turned out to be insignificant.) The British consul in Kerman, George Falconer, instructed by his government to hurry Reza Shah out of the country, assured the ex-shah that he need not await fund transfers since all his travel expenses would be covered by the British government. Reza Shah replied that the problem was not the cost of travel. "I asked for money for [living] expenses. I cannot leave in such a hurry." [5]

He feared being "strapped for money" in exile, he said.[6] Responding to a letter from his son while he was still on Iranian soil, he gently but urgently reminded the new shah that "you said nothing regarding the expenses of this large family abroad—as to from where, under what arrangements, and with what assurance the money will reach us." What he wanted, he wrote, was for the transfer of "a substantial sum" to a foreign bank, with arrangements for regular monthly payments "so that after arrival at our destination we can give order to our lives." [7]

In fact, Reza Shah did not remain impoverished for long. By the time he arrived at the island of Mauritius to begin his exile, Mohammad Reza Shah had arranged for two transfers totaling nearly £35,000 through Lloyds Bank and Barclays Bank.[8] Once in exile, Reza Shah received money transfers from his son on a regular basis. Moreover, the British government, the movers behind Reza Shah's abdication and exile, concluded they should shoulder a major part of the cost of his upkeep, at least during the Mauritius period. Still, money concerns did not disappear. Well provided for and parsimonious himself, Reza Shah's eldest daughter and older sons had extravagant tastes. Besides, Reza Shah had always displayed anxiety regarding his financial security. When in April 1942 the British acquiesced in Reza Shah's desire to move from Mauritius, which he found oppressive, to Canada, they also decided that he should pay his own expenses, adding (the British estimated) between £600 and £1,000 to his monthly expenditures.[9] Once Reza Shah died, the unimpeded right to his estate, including the substantial sum remaining in his bank account, became a point of contention between Mohammad Reza Shah and the Government of South Africa. Thus money, a focus of attention during his life in exile, remained an issue after his death.

A Voracious Appetite for Wealth

First, a bit of background is in order.

From the time he began his rise to power as a young officer in the Cossack Brigade, Reza Khan, as he was then known, displayed a voracious appetite for accumulating wealth—this despite the fact that, by and large, his personal tastes remained simple, even ascetic, whether as an ordinary soldier and an officer living in military barracks, or as the shah, inhabiting royal palaces. As minister of war and as prime minister, Reza Khan had demanded and secured a considerable portion of government revenues for the army while refusing to permit any outside scrutiny of the war ministry's accounts. Earlier, immediately after the 1921 coup, he and Seyyed Zia ordered the arrest of members of the old ruling class, demanding hefty sums for the prisoners' release—a demand that was at least partly designed to replenish a depleted treasury. Critics alleged Reza Khan was using extortion and military funds to amass a personal fortune. In a surprisingly frank conversation in 1923, Reza Khan told the British minister, Sir Percy Loraine,

> The accusation that he had pocketed any money is false. He had however on two occasions taken money not as bribes but by force from wealthy families. 70,000 tomans from the sons of Zell al Soltan [a Qajar prince] and of this sum he had spent 30,000 tomans on the military school and deposited the remainder in the bank … 30,000 tomans from Farmanfarma [another Qajar prince and major landowner] and deposited it in another bank … these two sums to provide for the future of his children … His own modest needs have been paid by the state.[10]

This early inclination to use office and coercion for personal benefit and to secure his family intensified after he became shah. He set about assembling for himself vast landholdings, not only in the agriculturally fertile Caspian provinces of Māzandarān and Gorgān but also in almost every part of the country. The acquisition of these properties was almost always accomplished through an official deed of sale or deed of transfer—but by questionable means. Owners were "persuaded" to sell at well below market prices or to "gift" their property to the shah. In property disputes and in the interpretation of imprecise property deeds, pliant judicial authorities issued rulings favorable to the monarch. Sometimes, property was acquired through outright confiscation—for example, of the holdings of rebellious tribal chiefs or of landowners accused of plotting against the state. State-owned land (*khāleseh*) was purchased by Reza Shah at highly favorable prices.[11]

An elaborate bureaucracy, organized into seven geographical departments, was established to manage the royal estates. Many of the overseers, agents, and inspectors were military officers whose salaries were paid by the army. These agents, eager to ingratiate themselves with the shah, abetted and even encouraged his acquisitions. For example, scattered peasant or small landowner holdings might lie between two villages held by the shah. Ways were found (coerced sale, judicial rulings) to transfer ownership to the shah and give him a continuous stretch of property.[12] Diplomats stationed in Tehran commented on Reza Shah's acquisitive instincts. The American minister in Tehran, Charles Hart, wrote that Reza Shah aspired to travel across hundreds of miles of Iran—all through his own property.[13] The British minister, Reader Bullard, commented on Reza Shah's propensity to amass property by forcing owners to sell at "ruinously low prices."[14] Revenue from these landholdings financed full or partial ownership of hotels, textile and silk-spinning mills, and a sugar refinery, but charities as well.[15] When he abdicated in 1941, Reza Shah was estimated to own more than two thousand villages or parts of villages across Iran.[16] Some sources cite even higher figures for his holdings.[17]

The Transfer of Property

On his abdication, Reza Shah ceded his carefully assembled and vast property holding to his son, Mohammad Reza Shah. He appears to have been propelled to take this step largely under British pressure and by the desire to preserve the throne for his son. The British foreign secretary, Anthony Eden, knew with near certainty that entry of British and Russian troops into the capital on September 16, four weeks after the initial occupation, would lead to Reza Shah's abdication. As noted in Chapter 3, in considering the future of the ex-shah, the Foreign Office had briefly toyed with the idea of deposing the Pahlavi dynasty altogether and restoring the Qajars to the throne, but that Bullard had advised against such a move and had recommended instead that Mohammad Reza Pahlavi be allowed to succeed his father in keeping with the constitution and in the interest of stability—but on condition that Reza Shah leave the country, take all his sons with him, and transfer his vast wealth to the nation.

The formal transfer of property took place in Isfahan, as the shah was making his way across Iran to leave the country. The task of securing Reza Shah's signature on the transfer document (*sanad-e enteqal*) fell to a prominent elder statesman and landowner, Qavam al-Molk Shirazi, whose son was married to Reza Shah's daughter, Princess Ashraf, and to Mohammad Sajjadi, a long-time cabinet officer and minister of roads in the first post-abdication cabinet. Both were men trusted by Reza Shah. Sajjadi writes that a few days after the swearing in of the new shah he was summoned to the royal palace and asked by Mohammad Reza Shah to carry a letter to his father regarding the property transfer. Sajjadi was unable to refuse the daunting assignment. Qavām and a reluctant Sajjadi left for Isfahan the next day, spent the night in Isfahan, and asked for a private audience with Reza Shah the following morning. They were received in the home of the prominent Isfahani merchant, Kazerouni, where Reza Shah and his family were staying.

Sajjadi described this dramatic moment in a subsequent memoir. The shah, smiling but ill at ease, received the two men and said to Sajjadi, "Oh, minister of roads, I know that you have come to send me on my way." He read his son's letter and put it down. "Very well," he remarked. "I, too, had such an intention. Bring me pen and paper."[18] It happened to be a Friday, when all government offices and notary public offices were closed. Sajjadi searched high and low for a notary and finally located one to draw up the legal transfer document. Reza Shah signed it. According to Sajjadi, he then drew a checkbook out of his briefcase and said, "All the cash I own, 680 million rials, is in my private account at the central branch of the Melli [National] Bank." He knew, he added, that once he set foot out of the country, "they will everywhere say and write that I put away countless monies in foreign banks for just such a day. But I can say unequivocally that I have no money in foreign banks or in any domestic bank other than the National Bank."[19]

Rumors of Reza Shah's alleged millions in British and American bank accounts did in fact begin to circulate after his abdication and were deliberately repeated on the BBC Persian language broadcasts from India, much to the consternation of the Iranian government. The BBC's harsh criticism of Reza Shah's rule began as part of the planning by the British government for the invasion of Iran and continued after his abdication. The FO, however, decided to drop allegations of Reza Shah's foreign bank accounts, for which there was no foundation. "The G[overnment] of India seem to have rather a guilty conscience on this matter!," minuted H. A. Caccia, a senior FO official. "There is no reason to pursue this issue further." I. T. M. Pink, one of the diplomats dealing with Iran at the FO, agreed: "The idea of hoarded millions in foreign banks was a useful propaganda point, but it has served its purpose and has become rather embarrassing," he wrote. The BBC Persian service was now instructed to "dispel the illusion" of foreign bank accounts, certainly insofar as British banks were concerned.[20]

In the Reza Shah-Sajjadi encounter, there was more to come. Reza Shah, it turned out, not only knew exactly how much cash he had in his bank account, he also kept a detailed record, village by village, and holding by holding, of the revenues accruing to him from his estates. According to Sajjadi,

> The shah then took out a notebook from his briefcase and handed it to me. The pages of this notebook were covered with a detailed list, written in pencil and in the late shah's own hand, of all [his] properties and movables. Beside each piece of property was noted the revenues it generated each year, over several years ... Reza Shah said: "to this hour, no one knew of the existence of this notebook. I had a right to keep it secret ... from the accountants of my estates, so that when at the end of the year they put the balance sheet before me, I would not endorse it without consulting my notebook ... It is no longer of any use to me. Today, I hand it to you to give to my dear son."[21]

Mauritius: Expenditure on a Liberal Scale

As already noted, the British did not expect Reza Shah to pay for his passage out of the country; and Skrine had already purchased rugs, stair carpeting, mattresses and pillows, bed linen, towels, and even dust rags and kitchen cloths, as advised by the governor of Mauritius, Bede Clifford. They now had to consider how to pay for his expenses in his place of exile in Mauritius— rent, food, general household expenditures, salaries for locally hired servants, entertainment.

Clifford's staff had also found a suitable house, Valory (Val Ory), in Mauritius for the royal family and had begun to furnish it. Clifford was instructed to meet the requirements of the royal family on a "reasonable" scale. With the family ensconced in their new home in Mauritius, Clifford cabled London for further instructions:

> I feel obliged to meet all the demands of the party and in doing so I assume I must interpret the word "reasonable" ... in accordance with their royal status. Judged by any other standard demands so far made would have to be regarded as very extravagant and in meeting them I have assumed that I must keep them as contented as possible.[22]

More detail was provided by Skrine. He wrote,

> Considerable sums were spent before the ex-Shah arrived in providing and furnishing houses for him and his large party, and since they came, heavy bills have been run up for catering, transport, P. W. D. supplies and services, medical attendance, etc. None of the family have any idea of the value of money, and any article or services for which they have a whim is ordered regardless of cost ... The *Governor has* sanctioned free of cost to the ex-Shah the provision of all the furniture and fittings [at] "Valory" as well as various articles which have been purchased on request since the party arrived.[23]

A flurry of correspondence followed between Tehran, London, and the Colonial Office (CO) regarding ultimate responsibility for Reza Shah's upkeep. For a time, the FO seemed under the impression that Reza Shah would be allocated a pension by the Iranian government out of which he would refund the expenses already incurred on his behalf and shoulder the costs of the future upkeep of himself and his family.[24] The FO even sent a cable to Bullard in Tehran to encourage the Iranian government to hurry things up. Bullard, however, dampened such expectations. He thought it unlikely that the Parliament would vote a pension for Reza Shah. The ruling shah himself had not yet been allocated a budget for his civil list and was living off funds left to him by his father. Since Reza Shah had funds at his disposal sufficient to last him a considerable period of time, he wrote, "I suggest that the difficult task of obtaining a pension for him from Parliament should be postponed."[25]

After some discussion, the FO and the CO arrived at a formula that held as long as Reza Shah remained in Mauritius:

Accommodation, furniture, food, <u>clothes</u>, motor transport, <u>recreation and other needs</u> on a <u>liberal scale</u> ... will be provided by His Majesty's Government, while goods which become the personal property of the ex-Shah or his suite should be paid for out of their own funds.[26]

Included in goods that became personal property were "luxuries such as additional cars, radios, etc."[27]

The Treasury grudgingly concurred. "That the British tax payer should have to find the funds for the ex-Shah is naturally not very palatable to us," a Treasury official wrote to the FO, but "since H. M. G. had to keep him in British territory and for that purpose sent him to Mauritius, there was no alternative to accepting the charge." The Treasury also decided the cost of Reza Shah's upkeep should fall on the CO.[28]

The phrase "additional cars, radios, etc." that the shah's family would themselves have to pay for requires a word of explanation. Skrine, it will be recalled, had purchased in Bombay not only the household goods the governor of Mauritius had advised that the royal party bring with them but also "expensive luxuries" ordered by family members, who were barred from going onshore to shop for themselves. For all these purchases, he presented Reza Shah with a bill for £3,260, for which the ex-shah wrote out a check against an account set up in his name at a British bank in India for the funds Mohammad Reza Shah had sent to his father.[29] These deposits were later transferred to a bank account set up for Reza Shah in Mauritius.

These arrangements meant that the British government bore most of the cost of Reza Shah's four-month stay in Mauritius, covering rent, the purchase of bathtubs, basins, and armoires, and other recurring expenditures for maintenance and repair, care of the grounds, salaries of extra guards, travel, utilities, and furniture rental.[30] It appears that they later refunded Reza Shah for the cost of the household items that Skrine had purchased in Bombay.[31] Reza Shah's expenditures on the island were not substantial.

Johannesburg: A Time for Economizing

Having agreed that His Majesty's Government should bear the cost of Reza Shah's maintenance in exile, they now also agreed that the medical expenses of the ex-shah and his party, as well as Tonking's salary, emoluments, and expenses, should be paid from the public purse.[32]An undercurrent of resentment at having to pay for the ex-shah's upkeep persisted, however. The Treasury, as mentioned earlier, acknowledged, but found "unpalatable," Britain's financial responsibility for the ex-shah. Skrine, describing the heavy cost of preparing to receive Reza Shah in Mauritius, had added, "I see no reason why the British taxpayer should be saddled with any expenditure on the ex-Shah and his party." The Iranian government, as the beneficiary of Reza Shah's considerable wealth, he wrote, should shoulder his expenses.[33] Other British officials shared these sentiments. Reza Shah's desire to relocate to Canada offered a means of shedding an unwelcome financial burden. The CO, the FO, and the Treasury concurred that, once settled in his new place of exile, Reza Shah should pay his own expenses. Reza Shah, eager to leave Mauritius, agreed.[34]

In South Africa, Reza Shah was not wanting for money. When he arrived in Durban he had £60,000 in his bank account, and periodic remittances from his son in Tehran and raised this figure to over £90,000 by 1943.[35] Yet a persistent sense of financial insecurity nagged him. For example, he initially wished the physician who had been attending him in Mauritius, Dr. de Chazal, to accompany him to South Africa. The FO balked at paying de Chazal's "none too modest fees," and even considered bargaining "to reduce them to rather less grandiose proportions." They decided that since Britain was paying for Tonking to accompany Reza Shah, the ex-shah should pay de Chazal's fees himself.[36] Reza Shah decided he did not need de Chazal's services after all.[37]

In choosing two houses for himself and his family in Johannesburg, Reza Shah had passed up the better residences that were shown to him, perhaps due to cost, though the family did later move to a larger house, with a five-acre walled garden in a good district in Johannesburg in 1943. Tonking noted that "His Majesty seems rather too careful about money matters, presumably anticipating a cessation of supplies from Persia." Yet at the time he had in his bank account enough funds, at current spending levels, to last him for five years. Reza Shah was also disinclined to pay tradespeople for their services if he considered them too high, risking damage to his good name, Tonking noted.[38] In early 1944, Reza Shah's private secretary told Tonking that the ex-shah "is being very difficult about household expenses and has been indulging in an economy drive which make[s] life very difficult for him."[39]

Parsimoniousness was not a quality ascribed to his three older sons, however. As noted in the previous chapter, their spending habits and "escapades" in Johannesburg were often a subject of exchanges between British and South African officials. Tonking wished to see the two youngest of the five sons sent home, "as he fears all sorts of trouble of the kind he had already experienced in connexion with the escapades of the older boys."[40] (The two younger boys were eventually sent back to Tehran.) The South African government wanted to avoid adverse press comment arising from the "gay time" the three older boys were having in and around Johannesburg and quashed the wish of the two older boys, Ali Reza and Gholam Reza, to spend Christmas at the Edward Hotel in Durban: "It is most undesirable that their Royal Highnesses should make pleasure trips or, for that matter, travel about the country at all under prevailing conditions," the South African secretary for external affairs wrote to the Office of the High Commissioner.[41]

Petrol consumption was also a problem. The boys had acquired additional cars in Johannesburg. Aside from Reza Shah's Cadillac, which he used little, the older boys had at their disposal a Mercedes Benz, a Studebaker, and three Buicks. Their gasoline consumption was high, and the South African government feared a public outcry, since war rationing was in place. A report noted that the royal family's petrol consumption rose from 128 gallons in July to 300 gallons in August 1942, and 340 gallons a month in November and December. Consumption continued to run at well over 200 gallons in some months in 1943.[42]

Tonking had his hands full with the boys: "Dr. T. is having his usual problems with the amorous adventures of the Princes, with which Johannesburg offers considerable scope," noted C. G. Sayers, an official in the high commissioner's office.[43] Replying to a query from Tehran, Tonking wrote that he was unaware if the eldest, Ali Reza, had any marriage plans, but the prince, he wrote, "is at present enjoying the favors of a blonde who, in her spare time, sells tickets at the Colosseum Picture Theatre."[44]

Ali Reza considered himself "Crown Prince" and next in line for the throne. A high spender, he was constantly having money problems. "Prince Ali has no money," and his bank balance was exhausted, the high commissioner in Pretoria wrote to Bullard in Tehran.[45] The manager of Barclays Bank in Johannesburg reported that Ali Reza had gone through £3,200 in twelve months and had less than £1 left in his account.[46] Tonking, who had to stand surety for the princes' bank overdrafts, did not want to see them run up bills. The problem, he wrote, was partly that the princes would receive lump sums from their brother, the shah, but that there was no regularity either in the timing or in amounts sent: "They are either rich or they are broke,"[47] he wrote in February 1944. The boys were hesitant to ask their father for money, and Reza Shah seemed to think they needed nothing but board and lodging, Tonking noted. He estimated that the princes required £200–£300 a month and suggested that Bullard raise the matter with the shah. "All three are now quite destitute."[48] Bullard spoke to the shah, and the shah again sent the three older boys lump sums of £1,000, £500, and £500 to tide them over; he also arranged for a monthly stipend for each of £30.[49] Tonking found the amount so small that he asked for confirmation. "The Crown Prince pays this alone to his pet masseur."[50] Bullard realized that the princes "will of course think monthly allowances inadequate but I happen to know the Shah is or soon will be in financial straits." He advised that, without indicating awareness that the shah was short of funds, the boys should be told that their brother was a constitutional monarch and lacked unlimited resources. They should assist him by exercising economy.[51]

His sons notwithstanding, Reza Shah clearly tried to economize while in South Africa. After his death, to resolve a dispute over estate taxes (death duties), the royal court in Tehran provided the South African government with documentation showing that between 1941 and Reza Shah's death in 1944, Mohammad Reza Shah had sent his father through bank transfers £132,000. When Reza Shah passed away, as noted earlier, he left £110,000 in his bank account. This meant that in the roughly twenty-six months he lived in Durban and Johannesburg, he had spent around £1,000 a month. This was not a small amount at the time, but Reza Shah was clearly not in dire straits.

There were, to conclude, two facets to Reza Shah's finances in exile: British and Iranian. The British initially felt responsible for the financial maintenance of a former king over whose exile they had almost complete control. They determined the country of his residence and the visitors, including family members from Iran, he was permitted to receive. They censored his letters to his son and relatives in Iran; they decided if family members in South Africa could travel or return home. They had assumed a financial responsibility, and they were exercised to keep the ex-shah and his family reasonably content. But British officials found reason to shake off a financial undertaking they found onerous once Reza Shah was allowed to change his place of exile, although in South Africa, too, British officials remained in control of his movements and the degree of freedom he would enjoy.

As to Reza Shah: he seemed to simultaneously practice both extravagance toward his children and parsimony elsewhere. There were the multiple cars and the Talbot Sunbeam, the gold watches, and the "toys" and indulgences he permitted his sons; at the same time, he attempted to economize on household expenses, remained reluctant to pay tradesmen, and experienced persistent financial anxiety. Reza Shah had been a very wealthy man before he transferred all he owned to his son; and from the beginning of his exile, he feared that he would lack the means to support the "horde" of family members and servants accompanying him, or that his source of funds from Iran would dry up. He therefore saw to it that his son continued to add to his bank account. Financial anxieties notwithstanding, he left behind a large surplus in that account when he passed away. Ironically, as it turned out, he was as well funded in death as he had been in life.

9

"A Matter of Political Expediency": The Settlement of Reza Shah's Estate

When Reza Shah died in exile in Johannesburg, South Africa, in July 1944, the South African authorities moved quickly to secure his estate. Tonking, accompanied by David Robertson, a lawyer appointed by the master of the supreme court as *curator bonis* (the court's legal representative and executor of the estate), and a sworn appraiser, went to his residence on Young Avenue. They made an inventory of the contents—listing everything from furniture, personal clothing, and military uniforms to a Patek Philippe gold watch, jewelry, gold coins, the gold insignia for shoulder epaulets, and even a pair of Zeiss binoculars. They noted the balance remaining in his account at Barclays Bank in Johannesburg. A collection of eight Persian carpets was valued at nearly £16,000; and a large collection of over one thousand Persian gold coins, a few of them ancient, was valued by a diamond merchant at £1,864.[1] The items of value were deposited for safekeeping in Barclays Bank; the furniture and clothing were left in place.

Reza Shah had not left a will. In keeping with South African law regarding persons who died intestate, the executor took steps to publish announcements in the press in the event there were unknown creditors and claimants. He proceeded to calculate the value of the whole estate, assess the death duties (estate taxes) due, and, finally, to determine the heirs and to distribute the estate among them. The entire estate, including cash holdings, was eventually valued at just under £130,000; the death duties, at 33.3 percent, and a small succession tax were calculated at £43,800.[2]

In Tehran, Reza Shah's son, Mohammad Reza Shah, the ruling Iranian monarch, had other ideas for the handling of the estate, and he was eager to wind up matters quickly. He ordered all the items, except valuables and Reza Shah's sword (and the Zeiss binoculars), to be sold and the cash proceeds, along with the money in Reza Shah's bank account, the gold coin collection, and jewelry, to be transferred to him in Tehran.[3] Sir Reader Bullard suggested a reason for the shah's urgency in pressing for the liquidation of his father's estate: "According to the Minister of Court, M. Ala, the Shah is very hard up for money," he cabled the Foreign Office (FO). Of the 678 million rials[4] in his bank accounts that Reza Shah had transferred to his son on abdication in 1941, the new shah had made a "loan" to the ministry of finance of some 400 million rials—a sum he was never able to recover, Bullard wrote, "and, in addition, he has squandered large sums on subsidies to useless newspapers and individuals." He was spending much more on personal and family expenditure than allowed by his civil list, and he was unlikely to secure additional funds for the expenses of the royal court from the Iranian Parliament.[5]

Legal requirements did not allow the South African authorities to comply with the shah's wishes, at least not without the permission of the master of the supreme court.[6] However, the British government was eager to satisfy the shah's wishes; and the master of the supreme court and the South African authorities were ready to be accommodating, insofar as Union law allowed. For a moment in September 1945, it appeared that a procedure had been worked out so that the whole estate could be handed over to Mohammad Reza Shah. But things did not turn out this way. It was four years before the estate was settled. And this only after vigorous efforts by Bullard and his successor as ambassador in Tehran, John Helier Le Rougetel; endeavors at the highest levels of the British government; the involvement of the South African prime minister; and, finally, an act of the South African Parliament.

The Problem: Death Duties

The crux of the problem lay in the payment of death duties, which, as noted, came to the considerable sum of over £43,000. A second issue arose over the executor's responsibility to distribute the estate among the heirs: the wife (or wives) and children. This obligation, which the South African authorities took very seriously, applied whether the heirs were determined according to South African or Iranian law.

The shah was adamantly opposed to paying death duties. He maintained that all the money and valuables in Reza Shah's possession were in fact his. When Reza Shah abdicated and was taken into exile by the British in 1941, he had ceded everything he owned—considerable holdings in land, factories, hotels, and deposits in bank accounts—to his son and successor. He in effect went into exile penniless. Over the ensuing three years, Mohammad Reza Shah had at intervals sent his father sums of money to allow him to meet his expenses. The shah now argued that everything Reza Shah owned at the time of his death should revert to him as "return to giver"[7] and that no death duties applied. As evidence, the royal court supplied the British embassy in Tehran with a notarized certificate and supporting bank documents showing that between 1941 and 1944, the shah had made transfers of money to his father totaling £132,000.[8] As to the distribution of the estate among living heirs, it followed that, if everything in Reza Shah's possession belonged to Mohammad Reza Shah, then inheritance did not enter the picture at all. The ruling monarch's brothers and sisters and Reza Shah's wife (or wives) were due nothing. So went the shah's argument.

The South African authorities were willing to accept the validity of what came to be known as "the deed of gift"—the notarized document by which Reza Shah had transferred his entire wealth to his son—and also to acknowledge that the money in Reza Shah's possession had been transferred to him by his son. They repeatedly affirmed they wished to do nothing to embarrass the British government in its desire to retain the shah's goodwill. The master of the supreme court, who had jurisdiction over all deceased estates, indicated he would accept a certificate by any relevant Iranian official (the minister of justice, the attorney general) that under Iranian law, the shah had legal claim to all or part of the estate. He was also ready to accept such a certificate specifying Iranian law on estate succession.[9] After the certificate detailing the funds the ruling shah had transferred to his father was received in South Africa, the executor and the master of the supreme court even agreed on a tentative procedure that would, in effect, have released the net estate, including cash and valuables, to the British high commissioner in South Africa for transfer to the British ambassador in Tehran for him to distribute among the heirs, including minors, "in consultation with the Shah."[10]

All these carefully worked out plans were upset, however, by a decision handed down by the South African commissioner of inland revenue. He ruled that the money transferred to Reza Shah became his. No condition had been attached to the use of the money; Reza Shah was free to do with it as he wished. His entire estate was therefore liable to death duties; and since Reza Shah died intestate, his heirs inherited. After consultation with his legal advisers, the master of the supreme court concurred with this finding.[11]

The shah unsurprisingly did not wish to pay over £43,000 in death duties. If the money were his, as he asserted, it also followed that the question of inheritance did not arise. In November 1946, the shah's chamberlain and a legal adviser succinctly put the shah's position to the British ambassador: "Everything that Reza Shah had in his possession in South Africa, personal articles or money, was property belonging to Muhammad [Reza] Shah put at Reza Shah's disposal," and any attempt of the Union government to impose estate taxes and determine how the estate should be distributed among the heirs was "beside the point" and "ultra vires"—outside the legal authority of the South African government.[12] The property should therefore "be released forthwith" by the Union government.[13]

The shah's preoccupation with this issue can be culled from the dispatches of the British ambassador in Tehran and also by the shah's repeated enquiries and the pressure he brought to bear on the British to persuade the Union authorities to hand over the estate to him. "The Shah is personally interested in speedy winding up of his father's estate and has more than once sent me messages about it," Bullard cabled to the FO in July 1945.[14] His successor, Le Rougetel, followed up with even more urgent dispatches. "I am under continuous pressure from the Court in this matter," he cabled in February 1947. "The Shah's Chamberlain tackled me again the day before yesterday."[15] In April 1947, the Iranian ambassador in London called at the FO to press again for an early settlement of the issue; and, as noted, the shah had sent his chamberlain and legal adviser to the British embassy in Tehran with the same mission.[16]

The Search for a Solution

The FO was not insensitive to these entreaties. On the contrary, FO officials continued to seek for a legal rationale to allow the Union government to release the whole of the estate to the shah without the payment of estate taxes. The task was complicated. The FO had to deal with the government of the Union of South Africa through the Dominions Office (DO), and the DO had to deal with the Union government through the British high commissioner in Cape Town. As a result, an intricate procedure developed: badgered by the shah's officials or the shah himself, the British ambassador in Tehran fired off urgent telegrams to the FO—his entire relationship with the shah was at risk, Le Rougetel repeatedly told the FO. The FO relayed these messages to the DO in London, sometimes in the form of pleas and suggestions, sometimes in the form of instructions. The DO, in turn, repeated these suggestions and instructions to the British high commissioner in Cape Town; and the high commissioner then sought to persuade the Union government to agree to a solution satisfactory to the shah.

This process continued month after month. At the suggestion of the South African government, the FO asked Bullard if the money and valuable items in Reza Shah's possession could be considered Crown, not personal, property and thus exempt from death duties.[17] But Bullard replied that such a claim was not possible: all the money in Reza Shah's possession had been sent to him by his son, the ruling shah, out of his private purse; and he wanted it back.[18] The FO then explored the possibility that the estate might be exempt from taxation under the principle that one state does not tax the sovereign of another state. They explored this avenue first with their own board of inland revenue, hoping a favorable reply might serve as a precedent for the Union government. But the secretary of the board replied that estates of foreign monarchs situated in England were liable to taxation. The sole exception to this rule, he noted, occurred on the death of Alexander III, emperor of Russia, in November 1894. Bonds and monies the emperor kept in the Bank of England were allowed to pass to his successor without incurring estate taxes. The secretary of the board took pains to add that the chancellor of the exchequer, who took sole responsibility for the decision, was "adversely criticized" in the Parliament, and that since then, in no case had the death duty on the estate of a foreign sovereign been forgiven.[19]

Despite this unwanted reply, the FO tried out this proposition on the Union authorities anyway—that a government does not tax the sovereign of another country. The Union government's reply was predictably not favorable. Foreign sovereigns resident in South Africa were liable to taxation. The only exemption had been granted to the King of Greece, who had taken up residence in South Africa following the German invasion of his country in the Second World War. Even in this instance, the Union authorities pointed out, special legislation was required; and, besides, Reza Shah was not a ruling monarch.[20] The FO continued to search for other legal arguments acceptable to the Union government for exempting the estate from taxes, including the special circumstances that led to Reza Shah's presence in South Africa—and also the proposition that Iranian, not South African, law should determine the ownership of Reza Shah's funds and other valuables.

The FO's persistence was driven to a large extent by the dispatches of its ambassador in Tehran. Concerned lest an adverse South African decision seriously damage his relations with the shah, Le Rougetel was relentless in advocating the shah's cause with his own government and in issuing dire warnings of repercussions should the shah be disappointed. Repeatedly, he called on the FO to press the DO and the high commissioner to impress on the South African government the desirability of a favorable decision.

"This matter had remained in suspense for two and a half years," Le Rougetel cabled in January 1947. "Further delay is bound to have an unfortunate effect on my personal relations with the Shah and is therefore highly undesirable on political grounds." Reporting on the visit of the shah's chamberlain and legal adviser who asserted that all the funds in Reza Shah's possession belonged to the ruling shah, Le Rougetel remarked, "It seems to me that in equity these arguments are quite unanswerable." He went on to urge that the Union government be persuaded "to release unconditionally and without delay the property in Reza Shah's possession at the time of his death."[21] Learning once again in early February 1947 from the FO that the Union government would not waive estate taxes, and also of its observation that, unlike the King of Greece, Reza Shah was not a reigning monarch, he cabled back: "A decision that death duties must be paid on the last Shah's estate at the rate of six shillings and eight pence in the pound [33.3 per cent] would I am sure infuriate His Majesty." He added, "Although ... the late Shah was not a reigning sovereign, tax in fact would be paid by his son who is."[22] Two weeks later, he pressed his case again: "The Shah does not understand, nor indeed do I, the attitude of the Union Government in regard to the disposal of the property which is clearly his."[23]

The efforts of Le Rougetel and the FO continued well into 1947, but the direction of these efforts was dramatically altered by the executor's final report, issued in late January of that year. The long report confirmed the finality of the decision of both the commissioner of inland revenue and the master of the supreme court and his law advisers that the Union law on estate taxes was applicable to the estate of Reza Shah. The report rehearsed the circumstances that brought Reza Shah to South Africa, noted the various arguments advanced for exempting the estate from taxation and the grounds on which these arguments were rejected, reviewed the relevant legislation, and finally concluded, "In the light of the above considerations it seems clear that under the laws of the Union of South Africa the estate of the ex Shah of Persia is chargeable with death duties in this country."[24] The executor's report did, however, suggest a way out. It added, "The matter therefore resolves into a question purely of political expediency. There is a liability to pay the tax in law: this can only be remitted by Parliament: it is for the Cabinet to decide whether or not it is desirable that special legislation should be introduced into Parliament to avoid the payment of the tax."[25]

The Legislative Option

This suggestion—to press for tax relief as a matter of political expediency—was quickly taken up by the FO in London and Le Rougetel in Tehran, but not before the FO pursued one last legal avenue to achieve the same end: the proposal that Iranian, not South African, law should determine whether ownership of the funds the shah sent his father remained with the ruling shah, as the Iranians claimed, or passed on to Reza Shah as determined under South African law.[26] Le Rougetel was now asked by the FO for "a full statement of the Persian law according to which [the current] Shah claims that he is still the owner of the property."[27] Le Rougetel refused to take this matter up with the Iranian authorities, possibly because he was well aware that there was no sound basis in Iranian law for the shah's claim that he retained absolute ownership of the assets he put at his father's disposal. The view that the ruling shah retained ownership may or may not be legally sound, he wrote, but "it is quite impossible for me to take legal advice in such a matter." If the Union government were not prepared to accept it, "we shall reach a deadlock which cannot fail to prejudice our relations with the Shah. ... If you insist on my pressing the Shah for an elucidation of the position in Persian law, I will, of course, do so but consequences may be most embarrassing both for me and for His Majesty's Government."[28] The FO now concluded it had exhausted all legal remedies: "In view of this telegram I think we must give up any idea of getting the South African authorities to reverse their decision on legal grounds and must concentrate on getting special legislation passed," minuted L. F. L. Pyman, one of the principal officers at the FO dealing with Iran.[29]

The DO suggested that a reluctant South African government might be prepared to ask the Parliament for special legislation to exempt Reza Shah's estate from taxes if it had assurances that such taxes would have been waived had the late shah taken up residence and died in the UK in similar circumstances. The FO now once again turned to the British board of inland revenue with a letter, written at the direction of the foreign secretary, Ernest Bevin. It deserves quotation as it makes clear how deeply the FO had become invested in the issue. The letter noted the FO's wish to persuade the Union government to pass special legislation in the matter of Reza Shah's estate. It stressed the "great political importance" Bevin attached to preserving good relations between the British ambassador in Tehran and the shah and the risk that these relations would be "seriously impaired" if estate duties were levied on the estate. Reza Shah's abdication in 1941, the letter pointed out, was precipitated by the Anglo-Soviet invasion of his country. He had not come to live in South Africa voluntarily. Britain had chosen his place of exile, first on the island of Mauritius, then in Johannesburg. It concluded,

> The circumstances in which the ex-Shah took up residence in South Africa and remained in residence there until his death were thus quite exceptional and Mr. Bevin trusts that in the circumstances it will be possible for the Board of Inland Revenue to agree that he may give the Government of the Union of South Africa the assurances referred to ... above.[30]

This time the board of inland revenue gave the FO the answer Bevin so clearly wanted to receive. The secretary of the board replied, as he had on a previous occasion, that the assets of an ex-monarch situated in England would normally be liable to estate taxes. However, if Reza Shah had taken up residence in England in circumstances similar to those in which he took up residence in South Africa, "the Board would have been prepared to accept the assurance of the present Shah that he, and not his father, was the owner of those assets. Consequently, the Board would have regarded them as immune from liability to Estate Duty in this country."[31]

The Appeal to Smuts

While this opinion was helpful, the FO concluded that it was not enough. The time had come to appeal directly to the South African prime minister, Field Marshal Jan Smuts, and to do so on the grounds of political expediency—the high interests of state. In May 1947, the FO asked John Stephenson, dominions secretary, to request the British high commissioner to raise the matter with Smuts. The letter laid out the arguments the high commissioner might use with Smuts. These arguments were incorporated in Stephenson's subsequent letter to the high commissioner: good relations with the shah were essential to retaining Britain's traditional influence in Iran; insistence on collecting estate taxes and on distributing the estate to heirs according to South African law could damage political relations between Iran and the UK; when the government of South Africa agreed to provide a place of residence to the exiled Reza Shah as a part of the war effort, it surely had no intention of subjecting monies sent to him by his son to taxation; Iran, moreover, had become a war ally, and it had provided the Allies with facilities across Iranian territory for the supply of war materiel to the Soviet Union; good relations with Iran were important not only to the UK but also to the Commonwealth, and Iranian oil went to all parts of the Commonwealth including South Africa.[32] So went the arguments to be put to the South African prime minister.

The appeal to Smuts had the desired effect. Things now moved fairly quickly. In July 1947, the South African minister of finance decided to waive death and succession duties on the estate "as an act of grace." However, under South African law, any remission of revenue in excess of £500 required a special appropriation by the Parliament,[33] and it was not until February 1948, when the Parliament was back in session, that it voted the funds to cover the remission of the relevant taxes.[34]

Another hitch had arisen in the meantime. In submitting legislation to the Parliament to waive death duties, the South African government had failed to request a waiver of the requirement that the estate be distributed to heirs as required under Union law, and the Union government was now hesitant, in fact refused, to submit another bill to the Parliament and "focus undesirable attention" on this issue.[35] This led to another flurry over many weeks of back-and-forth dispatches and consultations. By now, the executor was no longer insisting that South Africa law should govern the distribution of the estate to all the heirs; he appears to have been willing to leave this matter to the shah's discretion; but he was still insistent on ensuring that minors in the family received their fair share. The firm opinion of the Union government's law advisers was that the estate could not be released to the shah without an affidavit showing that, as head of the reigning house, he was the legal guardian and had control over the assets of minor members of his family.[36]

Le Rougetel, having already informed the shah that the estate would soon be released, was initially adamant that he could not ask for further documentation. He described the Union government's request for a formal affidavit as "pettifogging" and "most amazing."[37] However, the Union government insisted on an affidavit; and Le Rougetel finally secured it. It was signed by Malik Ismaili, acting both in his capacity as Iranian procurator general and as an expert in Iranian law. The affidavit affirmed that under Iranian law, the reigning monarch served as the guardian of members of the royal family who were still minors and that he was thus entitled to receive the inheritance due to them from the estate of their father. The affidavit cited by name the two of Reza Shah's children who were still minors.[38]

With the affidavit in hand, the Union government was able to release the estate to the shah; and the shah lost no time in taking control of it. He asked for all the cash assets to be deposited in an account in his own name at the same Barclays Bank branch where his father's account had been held and for a checkbook and a bank statement to be sent to him in Tehran.[39] He also asked that remaining movables from the estate be shipped to the Iranian embassy in Cairo for onward shipment to Iran. These included most of the items in the inventory initially drawn up by the executor and which had not been sold: jewelry, gold coins, carpets, Reza Shah's military uniforms, and the Zeiss binoculars.[40]

A brief comment on each of the main actors in this saga is perhaps in order. Mohammad Reza Shah was considered a weak monarch in these early years of his reign; yet in this instance at least, he demonstrated a steely determination to secure what he believed was rightly his. He was of course also in need of the money. As to the British government, its dominance and that of its ambassador in Tehran notwithstanding, it went out of its way to meet the shah's wishes in this matter. Clearly, the shah's goodwill and continued cooperation at a time of war mattered greatly to London. The Government of South Africa faced considerable pressure from the FO, but it remained committed to the letter of South African law. In the end, it found a way to meet the shah's wishes, but only through constitutional channels.

In August 1948, the British high commissioner in Cape Town received a copy of a bank deposit slip from the central branch of Barclays Bank in Johannesburg. It showed a deposit of £100,000 in the name of "Mohammad Reza Pahlavi, Shah of Persia,"[41] as an initial payment from the cash in the estate, with the rest to follow once all accounts were finalized. The long ordeal over the settlement of Reza Shah's estate had come to an end.

A Brief Epilogue

Reza Shah was one of a number of early-twentieth-century nationalist leaders and strongmen whose purpose was to modernize their countries and free them of great power interference or domination. He is often compared to Kemal Ataturk in neighboring Turkey, and the comparison is in many ways apt. Both men were military officers; and both lost their fathers (also military officers) in childhood. Both men rose to power at a moment of national humiliation, were fiercely nationalistic, and, as national leaders, believed in centralization, state-led political, economic, and social transformation, and Westernization. The changes they brought about in their countries were broadly similar. These included transformative changes in the system of education and the judiciary, the emancipation of women, secularization, and the weakening of the influence of the clergy. In both Turkey and Iran the Westernization and Europeanization efforts included the imposition of the Western hat and adoption of Western forms of dress and the requirement that all citizens adopt family names. But there were also significant differences between Ataturk and Reza Shah.

Ataturk was well-educated, having trained in a military secondary school and a military college; Reza Shah had no formal education that we know about and was largely self-educated. Ataturk, rising through the ranks of the Ottoman army, was already well-integrated into the Ottoman elites and reformers. Reza Khan was hardly a member of the Iranian elites, made his contacts with them late in life, and had little exposure to the West. That he in some fashion absorbed the "modern" ideas that animated Iran's aspiring reformers and pursued a project of modernization is therefore all the more striking. Ataturk, it is true, had to build on the ruins and the defeat and collapse of the Ottoman Empire in the First World War. Yet Ottoman reform in the nineteenth and early twentieth centuries had progressed much further and more successfully than reform efforts in Iran before the First World War. Ataturk inherited a state with stronger, better-developed military and state institutions than did Reza Shah. Secularization had already progressed further in Turkey than in Iran. At the same time, because the clerical institution in Iran was stronger than in Turkey, Reza Shah faced the more difficult clerical obstacles to reform.

Both men were in essence autocrats; but Ataturk abolished the centuries-old Ottoman sultanate and replaced it with a republic with himself as Turkey's first elected president. He left behind a political party that remained the elected party of government in Turkey long after his death. Ataturk also left behind a legacy that proved more open to the possibility of periods of democratic rule, free elections, and a relatively free press than did Reza Shah. In Iran due to clerical opposition, Reza Khan failed to abolish the monarchy and to establish a republic. He became not a president but a monarch in a long line of near-absolute monarchs. He tolerated neither an independent press nor an independent Parliament. For him, these were not institutions to nurture but talking shops that would only interfere with and hinder his nation-building project. The political party Reza Shah's court minister, Taymourtash, established proved fragile and of short duration; and periods of relative democracy and free elections in Iran in the post-Reza Shah period were of short duration. Yet the state structure that Reza Shah created proved durable and expanded during the reign of his son and successor. True, the 1979 Islamic Revolution did away with the monarchy altogether and vested supreme authority in the clergy and a clerical supreme leader; but the structure of other state institutions that took shape under Reza Shah—the government ministries, the bureaucracy, the state banks, the system of state schools, the ideal of a strong state spearheading economic development—proved remarkably durable across the watershed of the revolution.

Reza Shah was intent on ending a long period of British and Russian/Soviet dominance in Iran and their interference in its internal affairs; and to a large degree he succeeded in this endeavor. Yet, in one of those ironic twists of history, it was these two powers that invaded his country, engineered his abdication, and forced him into exile. It was in British hands that he spent the last few years of his life.

In exile, he was no longer the imperious, fearsome, relentless, driving force he had been when in power. As noted in an earlier chapter, an unanticipated invasion and occupation of his country and the end of his reign when there was so much more he had hoped to accomplish in some sense broke him. He went into exile almost meekly, always protesting but quietly surrendering to the inevitable: unable to choose his place of exile, confined to a remote island he abhorred, reduced to asking, not commanding, that he be allowed to live elsewhere. In a brief period of two decades, he had risen from the ranks of a simple military officer to the peak of power and had then become powerless, his freedom curbed, his choices limited.

We have noted his shortcomings. He was an autocrat by temperament and grew more autocratic during his years in power. He dealt harshly not only with unruly tribes and men and institutions whose authority could challenge his own but also with men who had served him well but whom he destroyed out of a nature too given to suspicion and mistrust. He silenced any semblance of a free press, controlled parliamentary elections, and turned the Majlis into a rubber stamp. There was more: he reinforced a tradition of absolutist rule, a habit of too-ready obedience to power by men in high office, and inclination of the population at large to seek resolution of the country's problems by the proverbial strongman. Despite an aspiration among many Iranians since the beginning of the twentieth century to democracy, representative government, a free press, and accountable government, his reign did little to strengthen the institutions that might have channeled Iran in this direction.

Yet his accomplishments were not meager. He took over a country that was economically bankrupt and politically adrift, in which the institutions of the state were weak, the ruling class ineffective, and the hopes of the reformists for a strong Iran with institutions suitable for the twentieth century dashed. He made effective use of very able men to build in the country strong institutions, a modern banking system, new industries, a judiciary system, a system of national education, and the idea that government should lead in encouraging trade, economic development, and industrialization.

It was a mixed yet impressive record. We can only guess how he judged himself—his accomplishments as well as his shortcomings—during his long, unhappy exile.

Notes

1 Soldier and King, Reformer and Autocrat

I have drawn for this chapter on the following sources: Ervand Abrahamian, *Iran between Two Revolutions* (Princeton, NJ: Princeton University Press, 1982); Ali M. Ansari, *Modern Iran: The Pahlavis and After* (Harlow: Pearson, 2003); Shahrough Akhavi, *Religion and Politics in Contemporary Iran: Clergy-State Relations in the Pahlavi Period* (Albany: State University of New York Press, 1980); Amin Banani, *The Modernization of Iran, 1921–1941* (Stanford, CA: Stanford University Press, 1961); L. P. Elwell-Sutton, "Reza Shah the Great: Founder of the Pahlavi Dynasty," in *Iran under the Pahlavis*, ed. George Lenczowski (Stanford, CA: Hoover Institution Press, 1978); Ann K. S. Lambton, *Landlord and Peasant in Persia* (Oxford: Oxford University Press, 1953); Lord Ironside, ed., *The Diaries of Major General Sir Edmund Ironside 1920–1922* (London: Leo Cooper, 1972).

1   Ironside, *Diaries of Major General Sir Edmund Ironside 1920–1922*, 138, 148.
2   Ibid.
3   Shaul Bakhash, "The Origins of the Anglo-Persian Agreement of 1919," *Asian and African Studies*, 25, no. 1 (March 1991), 1–26.
4   Elwell-Sutton, "Reza Shah the Great," 6.
5   Ironside, *Diaries of Major General Sir Edmund Ironside 1920–1922*, 161.
6   Elwell-Sutton, "Reza Shah the Great," 24.
7   Banani, *Modernization of Iran*, citing 1925 articles in this newspaper, 51.
8   Abrahamian, *Iran between Two Revolutions*, 124.
9   Ibid.
10 Ibid.
11 Elwell-Sutton, "Reza Shah the Great," 34.
12 Lambton, *Landlord and Peasant*, citing Millspaugh, 182–3.
13 Ibid., 286.
14 Banani, *Modernization of Iran*, 51, citing from 1925 articles in the newspaper *Rastakhiz*.
15 Houchang Chehabi, "Staging the Emperor's New Clothes: Dress Codes and Nation-Building under Reza Shah," *Iranian Studies*, 26, nos. 3–4 (1993), 227, 226.
16 From the doctoral dissertation of Ali-Akbar Siyasi, the later minister of education, in ibid., 225.
17 Ansari, *Modern Iran*, 55.

18 Ibid., 74.
19 Abrahamian, *Iran between Two Revolutions*, 150–1, 153.
20 Ibid.

2 Britain and the Abdication of Reza Shah

1   Bullard to Foreign Office, 595 (August 24, 1941), FO 371/27206.
2   Bullard to Foreign Office, 650 (September 3, 1941), FO 371/27211.
3   Bullard to Viscount Halifax, 3 (January 4, 1940), FO 416/98; and Annual Report for 1940, enclosure in Bullard to Eden, 37 (February 21, 1941), FO 416/99.
4   Bullard to Foreign Office, 202 (May 7, 1941), FO 371/27149.
5   Bullard to Foreign Office, 413 (July 7, 1941), FO 371/27150. Although Bullard defended Reza Shah's policy of neutrality as beneficial to England, he, however, continued to reiterate his view that his government should distance itself from Reza Shah should he be forced to flee as a result of German intrigue.
6   See, e.g., minute by C. W. Baxter attached to Bullard to Foreign Office, 397 (July 1, 1941), FO 371/27150 cited above: "On the whole, Iran's policy of neutrality … should not be altogether unwelcome to us."
7   Note from Viscount Halifax to the Iranian minister to London, Mohammad Ali Moghaddam (May 10, 1940), FO 416/98, p. 136.
8   Note from Moghaddam to Halifax (May 21, 1940), FO 416/98, p. 140.
9   Text in FO 416/98, p. 79.
10 Bullard to Halifax, 79 (April 15, 1940), FO 416/98.
11 Bullard to Halifax, 90 (April 22, 1940), FO 416/98.
12 Bullard to Halifax, 100 (April 27, 1940), FO 416/98.
13 Bullard to Halifax, 181 (June 20, 1940), FO 416/98.
14 Ibid. Bullard strongly believed in the efficacy of trade to win Iranian goodwill and repeatedly pleaded for greater efforts to meet Iran's import needs despite war scarcities. The Iranians, he wrote, saw England's inability to supply goods as evidence of weakness and Germany's ability to do so a sign of strength. See Bullard to Eden, 280 (December 27, 1940), FO 416/99.
15 Bullard to Foreign Office, 202, May 7, 1941, F0 371/27149.
16 Eden to Bullard, 179 (May 9, 1941), FO 371/27149, and Eden to Bullard, 198 (May 17, 1941), FO 371/27150.
17 Steps Iran took in response to British urgings are described in numerous dispatches from Tehran to the Foreign Office. See, e.g., Bullard to Halifax, 39 (February 6, 1940) and Bullard to Halifax, 89 (March 27, 1940), both in FO 416/98.

18 Iranian reasons for resisting large-scale reduction of Germans in Iran are
    spelled out in numerous Foreign Office files. See, e.g., the review of Iran–British
    exchanges on the German presence in Iran by C. V. Coverley Price (May 8,
    1941) and attached to Bullard to Eden, 202 (May 7, 1941), FO 371/27149;
    Bullard to Foreign Office, 216 (May 12, 1941) and the comments by various FO
    officials appended to it; and Eden to Bullard, 198 (May 17, 1941), both also in FO
    371/27149; and Bullard to Foreign Office, 495 (August 4, 1941), FO 371/27152.
19 Bullard to Foreign Office, 216 (May 12, 1941), FO 371/27149.
20 Memo by C. V. Coverley Price (May 8, 1941) attached to Bullard to Halifax, 202
    (May 7, 1940), FO 371/27149; and Bullard to Foreign Office, 397 (July 1, 1941),
    FO 371/27150. That the Foreign Office was at a loss as to what further to do,
    except remonstrate, about the Germans in Iran is reflected in a note in Eden's
    handwriting on Bullard's dispatch of May 7, cited in endnote 18. Eden wrote, "I
    have already stated my anxiety about Persia. What is our policy? What are we
    doing to give it effect?"
21 Annual Political Report for 1940, enclosed in Bullard to Eden, 37 (February 21,
    1941), FO 416/99.
22 Bullard to Halifax, 89 (March 27, 1940), FO 416/98.
23 See "Political Review of the Year 1939" enclosed in Bullard to Halifax, 17 (January
    17, 1940), FO 416/98.
24 Bullard to Foreign Office, 454 (July 22, 1941), FO 371/27151 (Part I of a three-
    part cable).
25 The letter (March 1, 1941) bears only the signature "C." It is addressed to "My
    dear Henry," indicating friendship with Hopkinson. The writer says he is a
    conveying suggestions by "my representative in Tehran," indicating a business
    connection with Iran. See document marked E933/933/34 in FO 371/27196.
    Hopkinson, the later Baron Colyton, was at this time the private secretary to
    Alexander Cadogan, the permanent undersecretary of state for foreign affairs.
26 See letter from Cadogan to Field Marshal Lord Ironside (March 14, 1941) marked
    E933/933/G in FO371/27196.
27 Foreign Office to Mr. Kelly (Berne), 325 (March 14, 1941) and 338 (March 16,
    1941), both in FO 371/27196.
28 The FO's cable to Miles Lampson (701) is not in the file but it is referenced in
    Lampson's reply. See endnote 30.
29 Ironside's letter to Cadogan, E933/933/5 (March 19, 1941), FO371/27196. Kelly's
    reply, 627 (March 22, 1941) E1090/933/34 in FO 371/27196. has been removed
    from the file and is embargoed to 2017. But there is no further mention of the
    Perron family in the correspondence on this subject.
30 Lampson to Foreign Office, 665 (March 22, 1941), FO371/27196. The reference
    to Freya Stark is in the same letter. Stark did go to Tehran later, in late April, but

remained briefly and there is no further mention of the "English maid" idea. However, that this whole improbable venture was taken seriously is indicated by the reactions in the Foreign Office to Lampson's reply: "This reply is also disappointing" (M. J. R. Talbott); "This offers little hope" (A. V. Coverley Price); and regarding the unlikelihood Stark will go to Tehran, "so, the idea of using her there will fall through" (signature unreadable).

31 The possibility, even likelihood, of a Russian collapse and the consequences for the British position in Iran was a source of persistent concern. For example, see Eden's personal note to Churchill (July 22, 1941) in FO 371/27230.

32 This is amply evident from the British records and became official policy. On August 10, just two weeks before the Anglo-Soviet invasion of Iran, still hoping to avoid the use of force, Eden suggested to Bullard offering Reza Shah a financial inducement to persuade him to expel the Germans. The offer is discussed in detail below. Two weeks earlier, the Chiefs of Staff Committee of the War Cabinet agreed that "our primary object should be to bring pressure on the Persian Government to evict the Germans if possible without the use of force." See War Cabinet: Chiefs of Staff Committee, Minute of a Meeting held in the Foreign Office (July 28, 1941), FO 371/27196.

33 Annual Political Report for 1940, enclosure in Bullard to Eden, 37 (February 23, 1941), FO 416/99, p. 9. (The FO 416 files consist of annual prints of selected correspondence concerning Iran, under the general title "Further Correspondence Respecting Persia." The page citations here and in the two subsequent endnotes refer to the page numbers in the print itself.)

34 Ibid., 13.

35 Ibid., 10.

36 Lambton to Bullard (May 1, 1941) in Bullard to Eden, 64 (May 1, 1941), FO 371/27150 (a print copy of the Lambton memo is in FO 416/99).

37 Ibid.

38 Bullard's cover letter in ibid. It was not unusual during the war, of course, for important documents to be shared with different departments and embassies.

39 Bullard to Foreign Office, 202 (May 7, 1941), FO 371/27149.

40 Bullard to Foreign Office, 220 (May 10, 1941), FO 371/27149.

41 See minutes dated June 30 and July 2, 1941, on the cover of Leo Amery to Eden (June 27, 1941), E3444/3444/34, FO 371/27230.

42 War Cabinet: Most Secret, W.M. (41), 77th Conclusions, Meeting (August 4, 1941), CAB 65/23, p. 2.

43 Eden to Bullard, 498 (August 8, 1941), FO 371/27197. Several days before he wrote Bullard, Eden had sounded out the Treasury on the feasibility of making "an attractive financial offer" to Reza Shah. He so informed his ambassador

in Moscow, Sir Stafford Cripps. See Eden to Cripps, 165 (August 4, 1941), FO 371/27231.

44 Bullard to Foreign Office, 523 (August 10, 1941), FO 371/27197.

45 Foreign Office to Bullard, 512 (August 11, 1941), FO 371/27197.

46 Bullard to Foreign Office, 524 (August 11, 1941), FO 371/27197.

47 See note to Eden (August 7, 1941) in FO 371/27196. The signature is difficult to read, but a penciled note and the contents indicate an Exchequer origin.

48 Eden to Bullard, 570 (August 26, 1941), FO 371/27207.

49 Prime Minister's Personal Minute (August 26, 1941), FO 371/27206.

50 Eden to Lampson, 2984, referenced in Lampson to Eden, 2665 (August 25, 1941), FO 371/27206.

51 Minutes by I. T. M. Pink and Henry Seymour appended to Bullard to Foreign Office, 605 (August 26, 1941), FO 371/27207.

52 Bullard to Foreign Office, 605, cited above.

53 Bullard to Foreign Office, 650 (September 3, 1941), FO 371/27211.

54 Eden to Bullard, 634 (September 5, 1941), FO 371/27211.

55 Eden to Bullard, 657 (September 8, 1941), FO 371/27211.

56 Bullard to Foreign Office, 717 (September 11, 1941), FO 371/27214.

57 Eden to Bullard, 695 (September 13, 1941), FO 371/27214. For a full list of the materials provided by the Legation, see R. Bullard, *Letters from Tehran: A British Ambassador in World War II Persia*, ed. E. C. Hodgkin (London: Faber and Faber, 1961), 79–81.

58 J. Gurney, "Ann Katharine Swynford Lambton: 1912–2008," in *Biographical Memoirs of Fellows of the British Academy*, XII (London: British Academy, 2013), 249.

59 Reader Bullard, *The Camels Must Go* (London: Faber and Faber, 1961), 229.

60 These assertions were made in a message for the American secretary of state that Eden sent to his ambassador in Washington. Churchill and Eden were anxious to retain the US support for their action in Iran. This telegram detailed other justifications for the imminent entry of Russian and British troops into the capital. See Eden to Washington, 5067 (September 14, 1941), FO 371/27211.

61 The editorial, titled (in Persian) "The Hurt of the Iranian Nation," is summarized in Bullard to Foreign Office, Tehran, 706 (September 11, 1941), FO 371/27213. Bullard first attributed the editorial to the crown prince then corrected himself and concluded it came from the Shah. See also Bullard to Foreign Office, 717 (September 11, 1941), FO 371/27215; and Bullard to Foreign Office, 746 (September 15, 1941), FO 371/27217. The publisher of *Ettelaat*, Abbas Massoudi, in an essay written many years later recalled the serious impact of the editorial on the Allies, but insisted that the editorial was an expression of the newspaper's own

viewpoint. He firmly denied it was written at the direction of the government, the crown prince, or the Shah. His essay is in Ebrahim Safa'i, ed., *Reza Shah-e Kabir dar A'ineh-ye Khaterat [Reza Shah the Great in the Mirror of Memoirs]* (Tehran: Ministry of Arts and Culture, 2535/1976), 347–9.

62 Eden to Cripps, 239 (September 12, 1941), FO 416/49. See also Bullard, *The Camels Must Go*, 228.

63 Eden to Bullard, 620 (September 3, 1940). See copy in CAB 65/23.

64 Wavell to War Office (October 29, 1941), E5203, FO 371/27233.

65 Prime Minister to Stalin, 1136 (August 29, 1941), CAB 65/23.

66 Prime Minister's Personal Minute to the Foreign Secretary, M.872/1, and Prime Minister's Personal Minute to Alexander Cadogan, M.868/1, both in FO 371/27211.

67 War Cabinet: Most Secret, W.M. (41) 89th Conclusions, Minute 2, Confidential Annex (September 4, 1941), CAB 65/23. A copy of the cable from Churchill to Bullard is attached.

68 War Cabinet: Most Secret, W.M. (41) 91st Conclusions, Minute 4, Confidential Annex (September 8, 1941), CAB 65/23.

69 Eden to Cripps, 236 (September 9, 1941), FO 371/27213.

70 War Cabinet: Most Secret, W.M. (41) 91st Conclusions, Minute 4, Confidential Annex (September 8, 1941), CAB 65/23.

71 Eden to Cripps, 231 (September 8, 1941), FO 416/99.

72 Eden to Cripps, 236 (September 9, 1941), FO 371/27213.

73 Eden to Cripps, 239 (September 12, 1941), FO 416/99.

74 Eden to Bullard, Personal, 682 (September 11, 1941), FO 371/27214. On the cover of the FO copy of this letter is a notation: "Yesterday Sir R. Bullard was given authority to discuss question of succession including possibility of Prince Hassan."

75 War Cabinet: W.M. (41) 93rd Conclusions, Minute 5, Confidential Annex (15 September 1941), CAB 65/23.

76 Bullard, 688 (September 12, 1941), FO 371/27213. See also the minute by the FO's I. T. M. Pink inked on Bullard's No. 706 of September 11, attributing the *Ettelaat* editorial to the crown prince and which served as the basis for Eden's cable: "This shows if any proof is needed that the Valiahd (crown prince) cannot be considered a serious candidate for the succession … this seems to dispose of the Crown Prince's claims."

77 Eden to Bullard, Personal, 682 (September 11, 1941), FO 371/27214. The Government of India and General Wavell, the commander-in-chief, India, also pressed for bringing down Reza Shah and restoring the Qajar dynasty. See Government of India to Secretary of State for India, Simla (August 29, 1941), FO 371/27209.

78 Bullard to Foreign Office, 746 (September 15, 1941).

79 Eden to Bullard, 729 (September 17, 1941), FO 371/27217. This telegram was sent after Reza Shah had abdicated.

80 G. R. Afkhami, *The Life and Times of the Shah* (Berkeley: University of California Press, 2009), 74.

81 Khosrow Mo'tazed, *Az Alasht ta Ifriqa* [*From Alasht to Africa*] (Tehran: Entesharat-e Dowr-e Donya, 1378/1999), 601. Mahmoud Foroughi, Prime Minister Mohammad Ali Foroughi's son, who was with his father, provides a different account of the moment of Reza Shah's abdication. He recalls that when his father, sick and at home, was given the details of a particularly harsh attack on the shah on the BBC Persian service, he rose from his sickbed saying, "I must get up … I must get from Reza Shah his abdication … There is no other recourse." Three hours later, Mahmoud Foroughi adds, "The late Foroughi [his father, the prime minister] returned … and handed me the Shah's instrument of abdication." See Mahmoud Foroughi, *Memoirs* [in Persian: *Khaterat-e Mahmoud Foroughi*], Iranian Oral History Project, Center for Middle Eastern Studies, Harvard University (Bethesda, MD: Ibex (Iran Books), 2003), 50–1, 53.

82 Bullard, *The Camels Must Go*, 230.

83 Mohammad Sa'ed Maraghe'i, the Iranian ambassador in Moscow in 1941, later recalled that when Hitler launched operation Barbarossa against the Soviet Union, he sensed from his conversations with Russian officials and diplomats in Moscow, including the British ambassador, Sir Stafford Cripps, that an Anglo-Soviet invasion of the country was likely. He had warned his government that the Allies desperately needed to use the Iranian railway and road network to supply Russia and would invade unless allowed to do so. He urged that Iran followed the example of Sweden, which had managed to maintain its neutrality even while permitting Germany to use Swedish railways for the transport of German troops. According to Sa'ed, the Iranian prime minister, Ali Mansur, was dismissive of his fears and, Sa'ed believes, never informed Reza Shah of his cables. When he later became prime minister, Sa'ed said he could find no trace of his cables in the Iranian Foreign Ministry files. Sa'ed's recollections are recounted by his son-in-law, Amir Aslan Afshar, in his memoirs. See *Khaterat-e Amir Aslan Afshar* [*The Memoirs of Amir Aslan Afshar*] (Tehran: Farhang Press, 2012/1991), 96–8.

84 Bullard to Foreign Office, 767 (September 17, 1941), FO 371/27217.

3 "Dear Anthony," "Dear Leo": Britain's Quixotic Flirtation with Dynastic Change

1 Amery to Eden, May 16, 1941, E 1872/933/34, in FO 371/27196.

2 "Middle East staff" is used in this book for members of what was officially known as the Eastern Department.

3 Minutes by Coverly Price, Baxter, and Seymour, written on the cover folder of Amery to Eden, May 16, 1941, E 1872/933/34, in FO 371/27196.

4 Eden to Amery, June 4, 1941, FO 371/27196.

5 Leo Amery, *The Empire at Bay: The Leo Amery Diaries 1929–1945*, ed. Leo Barnes and David Nicolson (London: Hutchinson, 1988), 698–9.

6 Amery to Eden, India Office, July 30, 1941, E 4276/933/34, FO 371/27196.

7 Amery to Eden, July 30, 1941, E 4276/923/34, FO 371/27196.

8 Minutes by Coverly Price, Baxter, and Seymour, May 16, 1941, E 1872/933/34, in FO 371/27196.

9 Bullard to Foreign Office, No. 520, Tehran, August 10, 1941, FO 371/27197.

10 Seymour's minute on Bullard to Foreign Office, No. 520, August 10, 1941, FO 371/27197.

11 Amery to Eden, August 14, 1941, E 4406/933/34, FO 371/27197.

12 Minute by Baxter on Amery to Eden, August 14, 1941, FO 371/27197.

13 Nicolson to Eden, August 8, 1941, E 4594/933/34, FO 371/27197.

14 Eden to Amery, August 18, 1941, E 4586/3691/G; Eden to Nicolson, August 18, 1941, E 4594/3691/G, FO 371/27197.

15 Amery, *Diaries*, 711.

16 The suggestion that, after a short stint as shah, Prince Hassan might be succeeded by his younger son is discussed in more detail later in this chapter.

17 Seymour to Private Secretary, August 26, 1941, E5316/3326/34, FO 371/27210. Amery had met with Prince Hamid that morning and noted in his diary:

> Then young Hamid Kadjar whom I had not seen for some time and who has developed into a most attractive virile young man. He earnestly urged the point that it must surely be to our interests after the war to have a Persian ruling family thoroughly English in its outlook … Personally, I would back the Kadjars, in spite of the incompetence of the two previous rulers, but Anthony seems very sticky. (See Amery, *Diaries*, 711)

18 Eden's comments are written on the margins of Seymour's note. See Seymour to Private Secretary, August 26, 1941, E5316/3326/34, FO 371/27210.

19 See, e.g., references to India's accusation of appeasement and references to its call for economic pressure, access to Iran's railways, and use of force in Secretary of State to the Government of India, Draft, July 26, 1941, FO 371/27196.

20 Government of India to the Secretary of State for India, 29 August 1941, enclosed in Amery to Eden, August 29, 1941, E 5261/3326/34, FO 371/27209. The Government of India continued to advocate the removal of Reza Shah. On September 4, Linlithgow cabled London: "We must have a Persian administration in being and a friendly population behind them. We can only secure this by

eliminating the Shah or by rendering him impotent." Government of India to Secretary of State for India, No. 4766, September 4, 1941, E 5393/3326/34, FO 371/27211.

21 Amery to Eden, August 29, 1941, FO 371/27209.

22 Eden's comments are written in his own hand on Amery's letter. See, as above, Amery to Eden, August 29, 1941, E 5261/3326/34, FO 371/27209.

23 Amery to Eden, May 16, 1941, E 1872/933/34, FO 371/27196. Amery himself also noted that the two young men were "almost too English for Persian purposes," but this didn't seem to give him any pause.

24 Eden to Bullard, No. 682, September 11, 1941, E 5588/3326/34, FO 371/27214.

25 Habib Ladjevardi, ed., *Memoirs of Prince Hamid Kadjar* (Cambridge: Center for Middle Eastern Studies, Harvard University, 1986), 44, 46–7. These "memoirs" are in the form of a direct transcription of an interview conducted by the editor with Hamid Qajar, and this may explain the sometimes awkward wording in the text.

26 Amery, *Diaries*, 714.

27 Inked note by H. A. Caccia, September 13, E5586/3326/34, FO 371/27214.

28 For Bullard's unfavorable assessment of the crown prince, see, e.g., Bullard to Foreign Office, No. 742, September 15, 1941, FO 371/27216.

29 Foreign Office to Bullard, No. 720, September 16, 1941, FO 371/27216.

30 Bullard to Foreign Office, No. 742, September 15, 1941, FO 371/27216.

31 This according to Foroughi's son, Mahmoud Foroughi, as described in the previous chapter. Then see Habib Ladjevardi, ed., *Memoirs of Mahmoud Foroughi* (Cambridge, MA: Center for Middle Eastern Studies, Harvard University, 2003), 50.

32 Bullard to Foreign Office, No. 746, September 15, 1941, F0 371/27217.

33 Bullard to Foreign Office, No. 767, September 17, 1941, E 5754/3326/34, FO 371/27217. The summary that follows is taken from both cables; the quotations all come from the Bullard's No. 767 of September 17.

34 Eden to Bullard, No. 729, September 17, 1941, FO 371/27217.

35 A second lunch that Nicolson arranged at his home so that Seymour could meet with and assess Prince Hassan did not go as well. "I fear my luncheon is not a success," Nicolson noted in his diary. Prince Hassan was "very charming but inconsequent," eager to leave London, before the air raids began; and when asked whether his younger son Hamid spoke Persian, he replied (the conversation was in French), "Pas un mot, pas un seul mot" ("Not a word, not a single word"). Nicolson diary, cited in Denis Wright, *The Persians among the English* (London: I.B. Tauris, 1985), 214.

36 Bullard to Foreign Office, No. 767, September 17, 1941, FO 371/27217.

37 The sources for this sampling of the diverse views of Foreign Office officials cited here are as follows: Popular movement to oust the Shah: Bullard to Eden, No. 64, May 1, 1941, FO 371/27150 and the enclosed Lambton memo; Chaos: Coverley Price's minute on Amery to Eden, May 16, 1941, FO 371/27196; Military officer or local leader taking power: Seymour's minute on Amery to Eden, July 30, 1941, FO 371/27196; Sweeping away whole Pahlavi brood: I. T. M. Pink's minute on Bullard to Foreign Office, No. 702, September 12, 1941, FO 371/27213; Possibility of a regency: minute by Pink on Bullard to Foreign Office, No. 627, August 30, 1942, FO 371/27208 and Eden to Bullard, No. 637, September 6, 1941, FO 371/27211.

4 The Journey into Exile

1 Khosrow Mo'tazed, *Az Alasht ta Ifriqa* [*From Alasht to Africa*] (Tehran: Entesharat-e Dowr-e Donya, 1378/1999), 601, 639.

2 Fereydoun Djam (Jam), Memoirs (transcript of interview), Iranian Oral History Project, Cambridge, Center for Middle Eastern Studies, Harvard University, Part I, November 24, 1981, 13 (hereafter, Jam).

3 Jam, I, 13–14.

4 Mo'tazed, *Az Alasht ta Ifriqa*, 606.

5 Jam, I, 17.

6 Mo'tazed, *Az Alasht ta Ifriqa*, 643.

7 The decision of the Argentine government to grant the shah and his entourage visas was reported to the FO by the British ambassador to Washington. See Halifax to Foreign Office, No. 4572, October 5, 1941, FO 371/27247.

8 Jam, I, 17.

9 FO to Bullard, No. 1075, November 22, 1942, E7544/5952/34, FO 371/27248. Such a form of words, regarding the undesirable elements that could influence Reza Shah in a neutral country, occurs often in British official correspondence.

10 Note from Amery to Walter Moyne, Secretary of State for the Colonies, September 16, 1941, CO. 968/46/10.

11 Government of India to Secretary of State for India, No. 5161, Simla, September 21, 1941, FO 371/27247.

12 Government of India to Secretary of State for India. Most Immediate (repeated to Tehran, Bushire Political Resident, and Consul, Kerman), No. 5163, Simla, September 22, 1941, FO 371/27247.

13 Secretary of State for India to Government of India, Most Immediate, No. 1173, September 21, 1941, FO 371/27247.

14 Government of India to Tehran, Secretary of State for India and Consul, Kerman, No. 5204, September 24, 1941 FO 371/27247.

15 Ibid.

16 This flurry of correspondence is in CO 968/46/10.

17 Clifford to Secretary of State for the Colonies, No. 512, September 25, 1941, FO 371/27247.

18 As noted in the previous chapter, "Britain and the Abdication of Reza Shah," the British had made clear they would acquiesce in Mohammad Reza Shah's succession only if Reza Shah abdicated, left Iran with all his sons, and transferred his wealth to the nation.

19 Princess Sham's memoirs are reprinted in Gholam Hosayn Mirza Saleh, ed., *Khaterat-e Solayman Behbudi, Shams Pahlavi va Ali Izadi* [*The Memoirs of Solayman Behbudi, Shams Pahlavi and Ali Izadi*] (Tehran: Tarh-e Now, 1372/1993), 406 (hereafter Saleh, Shams Memoirs); Ashraf Pahlavi, *Faces in a Mirror* (Englewood, NJ: Prentice Hall, 1960), 42.

20 For these observations on Reza Shah, see Mo'tazed, *Az Alasht ta Ifriqa*, 609, 612, 613, 619, 625–6; Shams, 409.

21 Mo'tazed, *Az Alasht ta Ifriqa*, 683–4.

22 Ibid., 613.

23 Ibid., 625.

24 Remarks to Harandi in Mo'tazed, *Az Alasht ta Ifriqa*, 648; to British consul, Saleh, Shams Memoirs, 411. A rial would have been equivalent to a few pennies. For several other references by Reza Shah to his lack of money, see Mo'tazed, *Az Alasht ta Ifriqa*, 613, 643, 648, 658, 661. The FO had agreed not to obstruct Mohammad Reza Shah's assuming the throne on the conditions described in Chapter 2.

25 Mo'tazed, *Az Alasht ta Ifriqa*, 626.

26 Saleh, Shams Memoirs, 407–8.

27 Mo'tazed, *Az Alasht ta Ifriqa*, 652, 653.

28 Ibid., 611–12; Saleh, Shams Memoirs, 405.

29 Mo'tazed, *Az Alasht ta Ifriqa*, 626.

30 Ibid.

31 Ibid., 647–8.

32 Ibid., 627.

33 Ibid., 647.

34 Ibid., 662. The anecdote of the three limping men is repeated, with variations, in several accounts.

35 Ibid., 663.

36 The FO had drawn up a numbered list giving the names and ages of the members of the royal party and accompanying servants who left Iran. In correspondence

between the FO, the CO, and Mauritius it became the practice, for the sake of identity and brevity, to refer to these individuals by their numbers. For example, when the royal party was already in Mauritius and some members asked to be allowed to return to Iran, the secretary of state for the colonies informed Governor Bede Clifford that two ladies-in-waiting would be allowed to return but "Nos. 3, 11 and 12" must remain in Mauritius. This was a reference to Princess Shams, her husband Fereydoun Jam, and the royal secretary, Ali Izadi. See Secretary of State for the Colonies to Clifford, November 13, 1941, CO 968/46/10.

37 Saleh, Shams Memoirs, 413; Mo'tazed, *Az Alasht ta Ifriqa,* 665.

38 Saleh, Shams Memoirs, 409, 413.

39 Mo'tazed, *Az Alasht ta Ifriqa,* 655.

40 Ibid., 681–2.

41 Copy of confidential letter from Falconer to Bullard, October 4, 1941, in Bullard to Foreign Office, No. 167, October 15, 1967, FO 371/27248.

42 A copy of the inventory, running several pages, signed and sealed by customs officials and addressed to the minister of finance, can be found in Mo'tazed, *Az Alasht ta Ifriqa,* 673–81. Reza Shah, angered at the accusations against the family, also insisted on a thorough examination of the baggage. See Jam, I, 17; and Mo'tazed, *Az Alasht ta Ifriqa,* 673.

43 Princess Ashraf (in Pahlavi, *Faces in a Mirror,* 42) writes she first saw her father in civilian clothes in Isfahan, but the other sources agree that it was when he boarded ship to leave Iran that he appeared in civilian clothes for the first time.

44 G. A. Falconer to Reader Bullard, October 4, 1941, enclosed in Bullard to Foreign Office, No. 16, October 15, 1941, FO 371/27248.

45 Saleh, Shams Memoirs, 415.

46 This scene is described in Skrine to Caroe, on the SS *Burma,* Bombay, October 6, 1941, FO 371/31393. This was the first of four long letters that, over the next three months, Skrine wrote to Sir Olaf Caroe and to his successor as secretary to the Government of India on his assignment to escort Reza Shah and his family to Mauritius. Skrine subsequently used this material for an article, "Assignment to Mauritius," published in *Blackwood's Magazine* (London, vol. 275, January–June 1954), 143–59.

47 In his reply, the viceroy asserted that the British government had "never agreed" that Reza Shah and his family should go to South America. But, in their own internal communications, British officials conceded that they "may have given the impression that agreement had been given to [a] temporary stay in India followed by permanent refuge in South America." These memos, Reza Shah's letter to the viceroy, and the viceroy's reply are in Government of India to Secretary of State for India, Most Immediate, Simla, No. 5449, October 4, 1941, CO 968/46/10.

48 Skrine, "Assignment to Mauritius," 147.

49 Skrine to Caroe, on the SS *Burma*, Bombay, October 6, 1941, FO 371/31393. In his Blackwood's Magazine article (p. 148), Skrine was more circumspect, writing only that the young princes "shook their fists" at the patrol boat.

50 Saleh, Shams Memoirs, 417.

51 Skrine, "Assignment to Mauritius," 148, 149, 150.

52 These details are pulled together from Skrine's "Assignment to Mauritius" article, 150, 152; and Skrine's letter to Caroe of October 6, cited in note 49.

53 Skrine, "Assignment to Mauritius," 149.

54 Saleh, Shams Memoirs, 422.

5 Mauritius: "This Is a Prison … a Death in Life"

1 Secretary of State for the Colonies to Sir B. Clifford, Mauritius, No. 478, Most Secret, October 8, 1941, FO 371/27247.

2 Secretary of State for the Colonies to Sir B. Clifford, Mauritius, No. 478, Most Secret, October 8, 1941, FO 371/27247.

3 Minute by I. T. M. Pink, Foreign Office, October 18, 1941, on Government of India to Mauritius, Simla, Immediate, No. 5616, October 10, 1941.

4 Skrine, Government House, Mauritius, to Caroe, Government of India, Confidential, October 22, 1941, FO 371/31393.

5 The description of Reza Shah's welcome at Port St. Louis, of the house, Valory (sometimes spelled Val Ory), and its furnishing, and the arrangements for catering and accommodation is drawn from the following sources: Bede Clifford, *Proconsul: Being Incidents in the Life and Career of Sir Bede Clifford* (London: Evans, 1964), 255–7; Clarmont Skrine, "Assignment to Mauritius," *Blackwood's Magazine*, 275 (January–June 1954), 154–6; and Skrine, Government House, Mauritius, to Olaf Caroe, Government of India, October 22, 1941, FO 371/31393.

6 Clifford to Secretary of State for the Colonies, No. 580, Secret, October 27, 1941 enclosed in E. V. Luke, Colonial Office, to I. T. M. Pink, Foreign Office, No. 13621/41, November 17, 1941, in folder 7485/5952/34, FO 371/27248.

7 Minute by W. M. Baxter on folder E 7497/5952/34 enclosing Luke's letter above, FO 371/27248. Words are underlined in the original.

8 Clifford to Secretary of State for the Colonies, No. 570, Secret, October 21, 1941, FO 371/27247.

9 Government of India, Simla, to Secretary of State for India, No.16580, October 13, 1941, CO 968/46/10, enclosed in E. W. R. Lumby, India Office, to Pink, Foreign Office, October 18, 1941, FO 371/27248.

10 Clifford to the Secretary of State for the Colonies, No. 612, Important, November 12, 1941, FO 371/27248.

11 Pink minute on Lumby, India Office, to Pink, Foreign Office, No. Ext. 65N/41, October 16, 1941, FO 371/27247.

12 Skrine wrote a detailed report to Hugh Weightman, his superior in the political department of the Government of India, regarding the action he took on these thirty-five letters. He listed the sender and recipient for each letter; and he briefly characterized the contents of each letter and the action he took on it. His report is included in Skrine to Weightman, Confidential, December 22, 1941, FO 371/31393. Skrine prepared a summary of the correspondence and precis of the contents of the more interesting letters for the Cairo censor and sent copies to the legation in Tehran and the governor of Mauritius.

13 Clifford to Secretary of State for the Colonies, No. 612, November 12, 1941, enclosed in Colonial Office to Foreign Office, November 14, 1941, FO 371/27248.

14 See, e.g., minute by W. H. Young (? signature unclear) on Bullard to FO, No 483, April 15, 1942, FO 371/27230.

15 A. B. Acheson, Colonial Office, to I. T. M. Pink, Foreign Office, No. 13621/41, October 1, 1941, FO 371/27247.

16 See Pink's comment, penciled in on Clifford to Secretary of State for the Colonies, No. 552, Most Secret, October 13, 1941, FO 371/27247.

17 Acheson, Colonial Office, to Pink, Foreign Office, October 1, 1941, FO 371/27247.

18 Skrine, Government House, Mauritius, to Caroe, Confidential, October 22, 1941, FO 371/31393; and Government of India to Mauritius, Simla, Immediate, No. 5616, October 10, 1941, FO 371/27247.

19 Clifford to Secretary of State for the Colonies, No. 552, Most Secret, October 13, 1941, FO 371/27247.

20 Skrine to Caroe, Confidential, Government House, Mauritius, October 22, 1941, FO 37131393.

21 Clifford to Secretary of State for the Colonies, Secret, No. 570, October 21, 1941, FO 371/27247. Clifford, in his memoir, was more kindly toward the princess, describing her as "one of the most distinguished women he had ever seen; handsome, with ... a very imperious demeanour ... She was reputed to have a violent temper, though whenever C. saw her she was gracious and dignified" (Clifford, *Proconsul*, 257). Clifford's book, though a memoir, is written in the third person.

22 Horace Seymour's minute on Bullard to Foreign Office, No. 1037, October 24, 1941, FO 371/27248.

23 All quotations from Skrine, "Assignment to Mauritius," 147; and Skrine to Caroe, Government House, Mauritius, Confidential, October 22, 1941, FO 371/31393.

24 Skrine, "Assignment to Mauritius," 154, 156 [and the letter above].

25 Shams Memoir, printed in Gholam Hosayn Mirza Saleh, *Khaterat-e Solayman Behbudi, Shams Pahlavi va Ali Izadi* [*The Memoirs of Solayman Behbudi, Shams Pahlavi and Ali Izadi*] (Tehran: Tarh-e Now Press, 1372/1993–4), 424 (hereafter, Saleh).

26 Khosrow Mo'tazed, *Az Alasht ta Ifriqa* [From Alasht to Africa] (Tehran: Entesharat-e Dowr-e Donya, 1378/1999), 325–7.

27 Ibid., 324, 327.

28 Ibid., 740.

29 Ibid., 427, 431. Her brother, Ali Reza, also remarked on these constraints and inability to write freely (Mo'tazed, *Az Alasht ta Ifriqa*, 745–6). Shams writes that until the Tripartite Agreement between Iran, Britain, and the Soviet Union was signed in January 1942, no letters or telegrams from Tehran to Mauritius reached them, nor were any of their letters or telegrams to Tehran accepted. But this cannot be accurate since Skrine's reports at the time suggest that, although censorship was in place, letters to and from the royal party in Mauritius were passed on well before this date, although delays were considerable.

30 Mo'tazed, *Az Alasht ta Ifriqa*, 430, 437.

31 The prince's letter is reprinted in Mo'tazed, *Az Alasht ta Ifriqa*, 742–7. Concerned that his letter would be censored, Prince Ali Reza hid it in a box of chocolates his aunt was taking with her when she was allowed to return to Iran.

32 Clifford to Secretary of State for the Colonies, No. 570, Secret, October 21, 1941, CO 968/46/10.

33 Clifford to Secretary of State for the Colonies, No. 570, Secret, October 21, 1941, CO 968/46/10.

34 Skrine to Caroe, Confidential, Government House, Mauritius, October 22, 1941, FO 371/31393.

35 Mo'tazed, Shams Memoirs, 437.

36 Ibid., 429.

37 Ibid.

38 Clifford to the Secretary of State for the Colonies, Secret, No. 603, November 11, 1941, FO 371/27248.

39 The description that follows in this and the next two paragraphs of Reza Shah's mood and feelings and the routine of his days in Mauritius is based on the memoirs of Shams and of Fereydoun Jam. See Mo'tazed, *Az Alasht ta Ifriqa*, 427–30; and Fereydoun Djam, transcript of interview by Habib Ladjevardi, Iranian Oral History Project, Center for Middle Eastern Studies, Harvard University, 1981, Part II, 4–8. Online at www.tel.lib.harvard.edu (hereafter, Jam).

40 Letter from Reza Shah to the Viceroy, as repeated in Government of India to the Secretary of State for India, No. 5459, Most Immediate, October 4, 1941, CO

968/46/10; and Skrine, on the SS *Burma*, Bombay, to Caroe, India Office, Secret, October 6, 1941, FO 371/31393.

41 Jam, II, 5.

42 Skrine to Weightman, New Delhi, December 22, 1941, FO 371/31393.

43 Clifford, *Proconsul*, 263.

44 "Report on His Majesty the Ex-Shah of Iran and Entourage from April 1942 to the Present Date," by H. D. Tonking, Mauritius, June 16, 1942, enclosed in Dominions Office to Secretary of State for Dominion Affairs, No. 211, Secret, FO 371/27230.

45 Jam, II, 5–6.

46 Government of India to the Secretary of State for India, Important, Simla, October 23, 1941, CO 968/46/10.

47 Bullard to Foreign Office, No. 1037, October 24, 1941, FO 371/276247.

48 Skrine, "Assignment to Mauritius," 148.

49 Ibid. 155.

50 Clifford, *Proconsul*, 256.

51 Ibid., 259.

52 Clifford to the Secretary of State for the Colonies, No. 574, Secret, October 24, 1941, FO 371/27248. Whether Reza Shah would have been ready to negotiate, as he claimed, had the British told him that they vitally needed to use Iranian overland routes and transportation networks to supply the Soviet Union is an intriguing question, but it is unlikely he would have agreed to what would have been a violation of Iranian neutrality. He told his son-in-law, Jam, he was determined to keep Iran out of the war; and anyway, it was not clear who would win it.

53 Caccia's minute of January 13, 1941 on Bullard, Tehran, to Foreign Office, No. 50, January 10, 1942, FO 371/31392.

54 Bullard, Tehran, to Foreign Office, No. 1037, Important, October 24, 1941, FO 371/27248.

55 The minutes by Pink, Caccia, and Seymour are appended to Bullard's October 14 cable, cited in the previous footnote.

56 See Bullard to Foreign Office, No. 1059, October 29, 1941, and Bullard to Foreign Office, No. 1131, November 15, 1941, both in FO 371/27248.

57 Clifford, Mauritius, to Secretary of State for the Colonies, No. 603, November 11, 1941, FO 371/27248.

58 See summary of Clifford's telegram on the folder enclosing India Office to Foreign Office, No. 7355/41, November 14, 1941, FO 371/27248.

59 Pink's comments, incorporating Eden's directive regarding the query to Canada, are handwritten in the folder containing Clifford's No. 603 of November 11, 1941, cited in the previous footnote. The number of the file folder is 7944/5952/34.

60 Cadogan to Machtig, Dominions Office, November 24, 1941, FO 371/27248. Almost the exact language was repeated in a letter that went directly from the prime minister's office to the British high commissioner in Canada. See Downing Street (signature not readable) to P. N. Loxley, December 6, 1941, FO 371/27248.

61 Foreign Office to Bullard, No. 1073, November 23, 1941, FO 371/27248.

62 Bullard to Foreign Office, No. 50, January 10, 1942, FO 371/31392.

63 Details on the debate in the Iranian Parliament over the treaty and the treaty itself can be found in R. K. Ramazani, *Iran's Foreign Policy 1941–1973* (Charlottesville: University of Virginia Press, 1975), 47–52.

64 Mo'tazed, *Az Alasht ta Ifriqa*, 431, 433.

65 Ibid., 444–6.

66 Clifford to Secretary of State for the Colonies, No. 206, Most Secret, March 29, 1942, FO 371/31392.

67 Young's minute, dated February 22 on Dominions Office to Foreign Office, February 20, 1942, FO 371/31392.

68 Bullard to Foreign Office, No. 474, April 13, 1942, FO 371/27230.

69 H. A. Young, Foreign Office, to S. E. V. Luke, Colonial Office, E 951/22/34, February 14, 1942, FO 371/31392.

70 Minute by Young, February 22, on CO to FO, No. 12621/42, February 21, 1942 in folder E 1201/22/34.

71 Minute by Young, February 23, on S. E. V. Luke, Colonial Office to Young, Foreign office, No. 13621/42, February 23, 1942, FO 371/31392.

72 Clifford to Secretary of State for the Colonies, No. 155, Most Secret, March 10, 1942, FO 371/31392.

73 H. A. Caccia's minute of March 16 on Clifford's No. 155, cited in the previous note.

74 For the complete medical report by the three doctors attending Reza Shah, see Foreign Office to Tehran, No. 487, April 9, 1942, repeating Clifford's telegram of April 1, 1942, FO 371/31392.

75 Governor, Sir B. Clifford to Secretary of State for the Colonies, No. 194, Most Secret, March 25, 1942; and same to same, No. 196, Most Secret, March 26, 1942, both in FO 371/31392.

76 Minutes by W. H. Young on Clifford to Secretary of State for the Colonies, Most Secret, No. 194, March 25, 1942, FO 371/31392, dated March 27 and 30. The Folder number is 1050270.

77 Minute, signature unreadable, dated March 27 and attached to Clifford's No. 194, cited above.

78 Further notes attached to Clifford's No. 194, cited above and Foreign Office to Tehran, No. 426, March 27, 1942, FO 371/31392.

79 Secretary of State for the Colonies to Governor Clifford, Most Secret No. 193, March 28, 1942, FO 371/31392.

80 Bullard to Foreign Office, Immediate, No. 392A, March 30, 1942, FO 371/31392, and Foreign Office to Tehran, No. 446, March 31, 1942.

81 Clifford to Secretary of State for the Colonies, Most Secret, No. 206, March 29, 1942, and Young's minutes of March 30 and April 2 attached to same, FO 371/31392.

6 Johannesburg and the Death of Reza Shah

1 Gholam Hosain Mirza Saleh, ed., *Khaterat-e Solayman Behbudi, Shams Pahlavi va Ali Izadi* [*The Memoirs of Solayman Behbudi, Shams Pahlavi and Ali Behbudi*] (Tehran: Tarikh-e Now Press, 1372/1993), Izadi memoirs, 463.

2 Clifford to Secretary of State for the Colonies, Most Secret, No. 195, March 25, 1942, FO 371/31392.

3 Saleh, Izadi memoirs, 454–5, 463.

4 See "Report on Recent Illness of H. M. the Ex-Shah of Persia," July 10, 1944 by H. D. Tonking, FO 371/40192.

5 H. D. Tonking, "Report on His Majesty the Ex-Shah of Iran and Entourage from April 1942 to the Present Date," Johannesburg, June 16, 1942, enclosed in Dominions Office to Foreign Office, No. W. F. 47/6, E 4747/22/34, August 11, 1942, 371/27230.

6 "Medical Report. re: His Majesty Mirza Riza Khan, aet. [age] 71. Ex Shah of Persia," May 26, 1942, FO 371/31393. May was assisted by Tonking. According to Tonking, it was Reza Shah's custom "to drink about two-thirds of a pint of brandy nightly and a bottle of red or white wine during the night," but since his illness had cut down his alcohol consumption to "negligible quantities." See Tonking's "Report on His Majesty the Ex-Shah of Iran," cited in endnote 5.

7 Minute by Young, dated July 8, on the medical report cited above. Reza Shah was reported to use opium, dating back to his days as a young officer in the Cossack Brigade and his military campaigns, but in modest amounts. The practice was widespread at the time and was believed to reduce fatigue and increase physical and mental resilience in times of stress.

8 For Smuts's evolving view regarding Reza Shah, see the following: India Office to Foreign Office, No. 7355/41, November 14, 1941, FO 371/27248 and Clifford's telegram in the same folder; High Commissioner, South Africa, to Dominions Office, No. 610, Secret, April 4, 1942, and same to same, No. 626, Secret, April 8, 1942, both in FO 371/31392.

9 H. D. Tonking, "Report on His Majesty the Ex-Shah of Iran and Entourage from April 1942 to the Present Date," Johannesburg, June 16, 1942, FO 371, 27230. Having taken Reza Shah into exile, the British government assumed responsible for all Reza Shah's travel and household expenses. Once he chose to live elsewhere, they shook off this undertaking, and Reza Shah agreed to cover his own expenses. High Commissioner to Dominions Office, No. 847, May 13, 1942, FO 371/27230; and High Commissioner, South Africa to Dominions Office, No. 1189, Secret, July 3, 1942, FO 371/27230.

10 Minute by I. T. M. Pink, dated May 15, on Dominions Office to Foreign Office, No. H. W. F. 47/8, May 14, 1942, FO 371/27230.

11 High Commissioner, South Africa to Dominions Office, No. 1062, June 15, 1942, FO 371/27230. South Africa's arguments for Tonking remaining with Reza Shah are culled from this and the High Commissioner's cable No. 1189 cited in footnote 11.

12 Saleh, Izadi Memoirs, 467.

13 Foundation for Iranian Studies, Oral History Project, interview with Prince Mahmud Reza Pahlavi, Los Angeles, April 18, 1985, 4 (in Farsi), https://fis-iran. org/en/content/pahlavi-prince-mahmud-reza.

14 Saleh, Izadi Memoirs, 465

15 Saleh, Izadi Memoirs, 469–70. Reza Shah's young son, Prince Mahmud Reza, recounts the crossing against a red-light incident as having occurred when he was with Reza Shah—and adds that because Reza Shah failed to heed the policeman, he and his father were even taken to a police station. See interview with Prince Mahmud Reza Pahlavi, Foundation for Iranian Studies, Oral History Project, Los Angeles, April 18, 1985, 4–5 (in Farsi), https://fis-iran.org/en/content/ pahlavi-prince-mahmud-reza.

16 British sources estimated Reza Shah's age when he arrived in Johannesburg variously at 72 and even 75. He himself said he was 65. The best documented Iranian source (Reza Niazmand, *Reza Shah: Az Tavallod ta Saltanat* [*Reza Shah: From Birth to Kingship*] (Bethesda, MD: Bonyad-e Mota'le'at-e Iran Press, 1996), 16), gives his date of birth as 1877.

17 These details of Reza Shah's experiences in and impressions of Durban and Johannesburg are based on Ali Izadi's memoirs in Saleh, 460–1, 464–5, 467.

18 Ashraf Pahlavi, *Faces in a Mirror: Memoirs from Exile* (Englewood, NJ: Prentice-Hall), 60.

19 For Tonking's reports on his conversations with the two men see FO 371/31393, "Report by H. D. Tonking on his conversations with Ernest Perron, August 25, 1942," enclosed in Dominions Office to Foreign Office, August 30, 1942, and material on Moqaddam in folder E6415/22/34 in the same file.

20 Young's minute, dated April 15, 1942, on Bullard to Foreign Office, No. 474, April 13, in Folder E2338/22/34, 1942, FO 371/27230.

21 See Annexure A, Colour Bar, in Tonking's "Report on His Majesty the Ex-Shah of Iran and Entourage from April 1942 to the Present Date," June 16, 1942, in FO 371/27230.

22 Saleh, Izadi Memoirs, 467–8. The quote is from p. 468.

23 See interview with Mahmud Reza, cited in footnote 13.

24 High Commissioner to the Dominions Office, No. 1686, Secret, September 25, 1942, FO 371/27230.

25 Young's minute on High Commissioner to the Dominions Office, No. 1686, cited above, FO 371/27230.

26 High Commissioner, South Africa, to Dominions Office, No. 1686, Secret, September 25, 1942, FO 371/27230.

27 Saleh, Izadi Memoirs, 470.

28 Tonking to B. P. Sullivan, Office of the High Commissioner, March 9, 1943, DO 119/1272.

29 Tonking to Political Secretary, Office of High Commissioner, for the UK, January 11, 1943, DO 119/1272.

30 The documents relating to the search for new housing for Reza Shah and the discussion regarding "Asiatics" and "coloured" occupation are in DO 119/1272 and DO 119/1273. The exchanges between officials in Pretoria, Johannesburg, and London discussed in the following two paragraphs mostly took the form of handwritten minutes or observations attached to one or two dispatches. The main dispatches cited here are in these two Dominion Office folders.

31 Tonking to Political Secretary, Office of High Commissioner for the UK, January 11, 1943, DO 119/1272.

32 Minute by B. P. S[ullivan], January 13, 1943, on Tonking's note cited in footnote above, and handwritten memos (signatures unclear) addressed to the deputy High Commissioner and the High Commissioner, dated January 26 and 27, 1943, all in DO 119/1272.

33 Tonking to Ben Cockram, Office of the High Commissioner, March 9, 1943, and note by Ben Cockram, Office of the High Commissioner, February 19, 1943, both in DO 119/1272.

34 Minute by B. P. S[ullivan], January 13, 1943, DO 119/1272.

35 Tonking, Johannesburg, to B. P. Sullivan, Office of the High Commissioner for the United Kingdom, Cape Town, March 9, 1943.

    Once the houses were vacated, the owner claimed that the princes had left their house "in a filthy, disreputable and dilapidated condition," and filed suit for the exorbitant sum of £700 for damages and repairs. See the letter the owner's solicitor, Max Franks, to Reza Shah's solicitors, Moodie and Robertson, of April 10, 1943, enclosed in Tonking, Johannesburg, to B. P. Sullivan, Office of High Commissioner, Cape Town, April 13, 1943, DO 119/1273. The Union government, asked for a legal exemption on behalf of Reza Shah, informed the high commissioner's office that municipal law did not exempt deposed or abdicated monarchs from the jurisdiction of the Union courts. There is additional materials on these claims and law suits, DO 119/1273.

36 Tonking to P. B. Sullivan, Office of High Commissioner, March 23, 1943, and Tonking to Sullivan, April 1, 1943, both in DO 119/1272.

37 Tonking to Sullivan, April 1, 1943, DO 119/1272.

38 Note written on the margins of Tonking's April 1 letter cited in the previous note.

39 See marginal note by B. P. S[ullivan] on Tonking's April 1 letter.

40 Department of External Affairs, Union of South Africa, to C. G. L. Syers, Office of the High Commissioner, April 17, 1943, and note signed C. G. S. to Sullivan, April 13, 1943, FO 119/1273.

41 The "escapades" of the young princes are described in more detail in the following chapter, "Reza Shah's Finances in Exile."

42 Department of External Affairs to C. G. L. Syers, Office of High Commissioner, September 3, 1943, DO 119/1275.

43 Dominion Office to Foreign Office, August 30, 1942, enclosing Tonking's report to the Political Secretary in the High Commissioner's Office for the UK on Perron's visit, August 25, 1942, FO 371/31393, and Tonking's follow-up note.

44 Bullard to Foreign Office, No. 933, July 23, 1942, FO 371/27230.

45 Bullard to Foreign Office, No. 1263, October 1, 1942, FO 371/27230. Tonking refers to Reza Shah's "marked aversion to any strangers being around him," in his report on the ex-shah and the royal family, cited above.

46 High Commissioner for the UK, Pretoria, to D. D. Forsyth, Office of the Prime Minister, September 15, 1943, DO 119/1274.

47 On Bullard's views: Secretary of State for Dominion Affairs, London, to the High Commissioner for the United Kingdom, Pretoria, No. 1035, August 6, 1943, DO 119/1274.

48 H. D. Tonking, "Educational Standards of Prince Ali Reza, Prince Gholam Reza and Prince Aborreza," in Folder 1020/420/43 in FO 119/1276.

49 B. Sullivan, Office of the High Commissioner, Cape Town, to Tonking, No. 1020/43, February 2 and February 21, 1944, DO 119/1275.

50 The extended correspondence regarding arrangements for the education of the young princes is in DO 119/1274. The problem confronting the shah in Tehran and British officials and the views of Lord Killearn, Bullard, and Ala are summarized in C. W. Baxter, Foreign Office, to Ifor Evans, British Council, January 18, 1944, FO 371/40192. The folder number is E 316/219/34.

51 High Commissioner to Dominions Office, No. 19, January 6, 1944, FO371/40192. The shah was reported to believe his youngest siblings "would be in danger" if they remained in Tehran, which Tonking understood to mean harmful to their characters.

52 Killearn, Cairo, to Foreign Office, No. 83, January 14, 1944, FO 371/40192.

53 C. W. Baxter, Foreign Office, to Ifor Evans, January 18, 1944, FO 371/40192.

54 Bullard to Baxter, E 7758/245/34, Confidential, Tehran, November 26, 1943, DO 119/1275.

55 Bullard to Baxter, No. 800, July 16, 1943, as cited in Baxter to Bullard, November 1, 1943, E6321/245/34, DO 119/1275.

56 Bullard, Tehran, to Baxter, Foreign Office, November 26, 1943, DO 119/1275.

57 There are numerous examples of the operations of this censorship in DO 119/1275; and Tonking, in his report on the ex-shah and family of June 1942, cited above, noted that "all cables and letters have been censored and copies kept."

58 Minute by H. D. Young, dated July 13, on Bullard to Foreign Office, No. 681, July 11, 1944, FO 371/40192. Perron and Princess Ashraf had come and gone by then. The folder number is E4110/219/34.

59 The instructions to Bullard are repeated in Secretary of State for Dominion Affairs to the High Commissioner for the United Kingdom, No. 620, Secret, Pretoria, June 22, 1944, FO 371/40192.

60 Young's minute on the dispatch cited in the preceding footnote.

61 Saleh, Izadi Memoirs, 473–4. Prince Mahmud Reza, however, recalled that the whole family ate lunch together, while Reza Shah had his dinner alone.

62 A letter from Reza Shah to Shams, in Khosrow Mo'tazed, *Az Alasht ta Ifriqa* [*From Alasht to Africa*] (Tehran: Entesharat-e Dowr-e Donya, 1378/1999), 847.

63 Several such letters from the Iranian archives appear in Mo'tazed's *Az Alasht.*

64 Tonking, Johannesburg, to B. P. Sullivan, Office of High Commissioner, Pretoria, July 6, 1943, DO 119/1274.

65 Secretary of State for Dominion Affairs, London, to High Commissioner for the United Kingdom in South Africa, Pretoria, Secret, July 13, 1943, DO 119/1274.

66 H. D. Tonking, "Report on H. M. the Ex-Shah of Iran," November 15, 1943, DO 119/1274. Tonking also noted that Reza Shah had led a hard life, smoked and drank heavily, and was drinking more heavily in the evenings than in the past.

67 Bullard to Baxter, No. G 176/3/44, Tehran, January 10, 1944, FO 371/40192.

68 C. W. Baxter, Foreign Office to H. E. Costar, Dominion Office, E565/216/34, January 31, 1944. This language was incorporated in a dispatch to the Dominions Office. See J. E. Stephenson, Dominions Office, to C. G. L. Syers, High Commissioner, WF 288/10, Secret, February 9, 1944, FO 371/40192.

69 Tonking, Johannesburg, to B. P. Sullivan, Office of the High Commissioner, Pretoria, Ref. 1020/43, March 20, 1944, DO 119/1274.

70 High Commissioner, South Africa, to Secretary of State for Dominion Affairs, No. 359, Secret, March 24, 1944, FO 371/40192.

71 W. H. Young, Foreign Office, to H. B. M. Staples, Dominions Office, April 1, 1944; and the minute (signature unclear) on the High Commissioner's No. 359, cited above. This language was incorporated in Dominion Office to High Commissioner, No. 345, Secret, April 7, 1944, both in FO 371/40192.

72 H. D. Tonking to B. P. Sullivan, Cape Town, Secret, April 29, 1944, FO 371/40192.

73 Saleh, Izadi Memoirs, 478.

74 H. D. Tonking, "Report on Recent Illness of H. M. the Ex-Shah of Iran," July 10, 1944, enclosed in Lascelles, Tehran, No. 9176/50/44, in Folder E 4910/219/34, FO 371/40193.

75 Saleh, Izadi Memoirs, 480. Reza Shah's last moments are also described in H. D. Tonking, "Report on the Death of H. M. the Ex-Shah of Iran," September 9, 1944, Folder 1020/448/43, DO 119/1276.

7 Wrapping Up

1   For the details on the handling and final settlement of Reza Shah's estate, see the following chapter.

2   For these details, see Tonking's "Report on the Death of H. M. the Ex Shah of Iran," DO 119/1276. The report is undated but must have been sent to the Dominions Office toward the end of September 1944.

3   Foreign Office Minute, July 27, 1944, FO 371/40192.

4   Peterson to Lascelles, July 27, 1942, and minute by Young, July 28, 1944, on same, FO 371/40192.

5   Peterson to Lascelles, July 30, 1944, F0 371/40192.

6   Lascelles, Tehran, to Foreign Office, No. 731, July 28, 1944, FO 371/40192, and same to same, No. 801, August 15, 1944, FO 371/40193. The signature on the Foreign Office minute, dated August 16, is not readable (Young?).

7   Foreign Office to Tehran, No. 519, August 17, 1944, FO 371/40193.

8   Lascelles to Foreign Office, NO. 801, August 15, 1944, fo 371/40193.

9   Foreign Office to Tehran, No. 519, August 17, 1944, FO 371/40193.

10 Foreign Office to Tehran, No. 519, August 17, 1944, and Lascelles to Foreign Office, No. 827A, August 22, 1944, both in FO 371/40193.

11 Lascelles to Foreign Office, No. 801, August 15, and same to same, No. 827A, August 22, 1944, both in FO 371/40193.

12 Foreign Office [Eden] to Tehran, No. 551, August 28, 1944, FO 371/40193.

13 Bullard to Foreign Office, No. 1050, October 13, 1944, FO 371/40193.

14 Bullard had been earlier instructed to persuade the Iranian Court to agree to sea passage and he appears to have eventually succeeded in doing so. See DO to Acting High Commissioner, South Africa, No. WF. 277/10, August 29, 1944, and Foreign Office to Tehran, No. 561, August 31, 1944, FO 371/40192.

15 Cairo to Foreign Office, No. 1290, November 2, 1944, FO 371/40193. Enclosed is a clipping from the *Journal d'Egypte* of October 29, 1944. For a similar account of these ceremonies, see a memoir by Reza Shah's son, Gholam Reza, who was present. It is cited in Reza Niazmand, *Reza Shah: as Suqut ta Marg* [Reza Shah: From Fall to Death] (Tehran: Hekayyat-e Qalam-e Novin Press, 1386/2007), 582–3.

16 High Commissioner, Pretoria, to Foreign Office, No. Q.0393, enclosed in Foreign Office to Tehran, No. 450, July 27, 1944, FO 371/40192; and Foreign Office to Tehran, No. 561, August 31, 1944, FO 371/40193.

17 Killearn to Foreign Office, No. 1676, August 27, 1944, FO 371/40193.

18 Ibid.

19 B. Staple, Dominions Office, to Young, Foreign Office, WF.288/17, November 25, 1944, FO 371/40193.

20 The reception ceremonies are detailed in Khosrow Mo'tazed, Az Alasht ta Ifriqa [From Alasht to Africa] (Tehran: Dowr-e Donya Press), 989–90.

8 "Where Do I Go without Money?" Reza Shah's Finances in Exile

1 The pound/dollar conversion is based on 1944 rates. The 2015 purchasing power of these amounts is based on an annual inflation rate of about 3.8 percent. For these calculations, see tables accessible at http://www.measuringworth.com.

2 The 1941 exchange rate was 68.8 rials to the British pound. The £9.8 million would have come to $29 million at the time.

3 Mo'tazed, Khosrow, *Az Ālāsht ta Ifriqā [From Ālāsht to Africa]* (Tehran: Enteshārāt-e Dowr-e Donyā, 1278/1999), 64. Mo'tazed has brought together in his book the memoirs of several of the participants in the events following Reza Shah's abdication and exile.

4 Ibid., 647.

5 Ibid., 648.

6 Ibid., 658.

7 Ibid., 661–2.

8 These transfers were tracked and reported by British officials. See FO 371/27248, Clifford to Secretary of State for the Colonies, No. 612, November 12, 1941, enclosed in Colonial Office to Foreign Office, November 14, 1941; and FO 371/27247, Reader Bullard to Foreign Office, No. 925, October 6, 1941, and also the minute on this dispatch by I. T. M. Pink, dated October 18, 1941.

9 Dominions Office (DO) 119/1274, "Report on H. M. the Ex-Shah of Iran," November 15, 1943, by H. M. Tonking.

10 Cyrus Ghani, *Iran and the Rise of Reza Shah* (London: I.B. Tauris, 1998), 205-6.

11 For these methods of property acquisition, see Ervand Abrahamian, *Iran between Two Revolutions* (Princeton, NJ: Princeton University Press, 1982), 137; A. K. S.Lambton, *The Persian Land Reform, 1962–1966* (Oxford: Clarendon Press, 1969), 49-50; and A. K. S.Lambton, *Landlord and Peasant in Persia* (Oxford: Oxford University Press), 256-7.

12 Memoirs of Ali-Akbar Derakhshāni, quoted in Moʿtazed, *Az Ālāsht ta Ifriqā*, 152-8. Derakhshani was a military officer who under Reza Shah served variously as governor of East Azerbaijan, commander of the Tabriz army, and an inspector for the royal estates. He provides interesting details on how the royal estates were managed and provides examples of the ways in which local agents and officials added to Reza Shah's properties.

13 Cited in Mohammad Gholi Majd, *Great Britain and Reza Shah: The Plunder of Iran* (Miami: University Press of Florida, 2001), 146.

14 Annual Political Report for 1940, enclosure in Bullard to Eden, February 23, 1941, FO 371/27150.

15 Abrahamian, *Iran between Two Revolutions*, 137; Majd, *Great Britain and Reza Shah*, 160-1.

16 Lambton, *The Persian Land Reform*, 49-50. Lambton is citing a post-abdication September 1941 royal decree and subsequent laws by which these properties were returned, under special procedures, to their original owners.

17 Moʿtazed, *Az Ālāsht ta Ifriqā*, 150-1. Moʿtazed cites archival records that became accessible after the Islamic revolution of 1979, which list over 6,000 "units" (*raqabeh*) of land owned in various districts of the country by Reza Shah, but it is not clear how the term *raqabeh* is being used here: probably it refers to parcels of land rather than to entire villages.

18 Moʿtazed, quoting Sajjadi's memoir, 622-3.

19 Ibid., 624.

20 Caccia, minute dated October 8 on India Office telegram no. 5500 of October 7, 1941, E 6513/5952/34; Pink minute dated October 12 on Bullard to Foreign Office, No. 954, October 9, 1941, E 6526/5952/34 FO 371/27248.

21 Moʿtazed, Sajjadi's Memoir, quoted in 624-5.

22 Sir B. Clifford to Secretary of State for the Colonies, No. 586, Most Secret, October 29, 1941, FO 371/27248.

23 "Note on the financial questions raised by the detention of the ex-Shah and his party in Mauritius," enclosed in Skrine to Caroe, Government House, Mauritius, October 30, 1941, FO 371/27230,

24 Foreign Office to S. E. V. Luke, Colonial Office, November 8, 1941, FO 371/27248.

25 Bullard, Tehran, to Foreign Office, No. 1198, November 23, 1941, FO 371/27248.

26 Colonial Office to I. T. M Pink, Foreign Office, 13621/41, December 18, 1941. Underlined words are in the original, FO 371/27248.

27 S. E. V. Luke, Colonial Office, to I. T. M. Pink, Foreign Office, No. 13621/41, December 18, 1941, E 846D/5952/34. The term "on a reasonable scale" was amended here to "on a liberal scale." See also Clifford to Secretary of State for the Colonies, No. 586, Most Secret, October 29, 1941, FO 371/27248.

28 C. G. L. Syers, Treasury Chambers, to W. H. Young, Foreign Office, December 10, 1941, E 5216/ 5952.34, FO 371/27248.

29 Clarmont Skrine, "Assignment to Mauritius," *Blackwood's Magazine*, No. 275 (January–June 1954), 149–50; and Skrine to Government of India, Secret, on the S. S. Burma, Bombay, October 6, 1941. The cost of the purchases Skrine gives in the article he wrote some years after these events is £3,650; and he speaks of five Persian carpets in his original report and of four carpets in his later article.

30 Clifford's report, which may not include all expenses, is in British National Archives, Colonial Office (CO) 968/107/5.

31 This is implicit in the enclosure in Skrine to Caroe, Mauritius, October 30, 1941, FO 371/27230, and by Clifford's observation (Clifford to Secretary of State for the Colonies, October 29, 1941, FO 371/27248). He wrote that the articles he mentioned and other supplies purchased by Skrine "with the shah's own money" will have to be refunded. The phrase "additional cars, radios, etc." cited in note 28 suggests Reza Shah was repaid for some of these purchases but would have to pay for any additional ones.

32 Folders E 5855/22/34 and E 6305/22/34, FO 371/31393.

33 "Note on the financial questions raised by the detention of the ex-Shah and his party in Mauritius," enclosed in Skrine to Caroe, Government House, Mauritius, October 30, 1941, FO 371/27230.

34 C. G. L. Syers, Treasury Chambers, to I. T. M. Pink, Foreign Office, January 2, 1942; and Clifford to Secretary of State for the Colonies, no. 79, Most Secret, February 6, 1942, FO 371/31392.

35 Note by B. P. S. on conversation with Tonking, January 13, 1943; and DO 119/1274, H. D. Tonking: Report on H. M. the Ex-Shah of Iran, November 15, 1943, DO 119/1272.

36 Foreign Office to S. E. V. Luke, Colonial Office, March 30, 1942, FO 371/31393.

37 Clifford to Secretary of State for the Colonies, No. 223, Most Secret, April 8, 1942, FO 371/31393.

38 Report by H. D. Tonking on his conversation with Ernest Perron, August 25, 1942, enclosed in Dominions Office to Foreign Office, August 30, 194 FO 371/31393.

39 Tonking to Sullivan, March 6, 1944, DO 119/1275.

40 High Commissioner for the UK, Pretoria, to Secretary of State for the Dominions, July 12, 1943, DO 119/1274.

41 Secretary of State for External Affairs to High Commissioner, November 29, 1943, DO 119/1274.

42 The petrol consumption report is in DO 119/1274. Minute by Sayers, June 3, 1944 DO 119/1275.

43 Minute by Sayers, June 3, 1944, in DO 119/1275.

44 Tonking to Sullivan, Secret, February 4, 1944, 1020/264/2, DO 119/1275.

45 High Commissioner for the UK, Pretoria, to Bullard, August 13, 1941. For clarity, I corrected an obvious typographical error. The original read: "Prince Ali has not money," DO 119/1275.

46 His Majesty's Trade Commissioner's Office (signature unreadable) to Sullivan, Office of High Commissioner, Pretoria, August 21, 1943, DO 119/1274.

47 Tonking to Sullivan, Officer of High Commissioner, cited in High Commissioner to Bullard, February 12, 1944, DO 119/1275.

48 High Commissioner to Bullard, February 12, 1944, DO 119/1275.

49 Secretary of State for Dominion Affairs, London, to High Commissioner, Pretoria, April 12, 1944, enclosing Bullard's No. 355 to Foreign Office, DO 119/1275.

50 Note by C. G. S[ayers], June 2, 1944, DO 119/1275.

51 Secretary of State for Dominion Affairs, London, to the High Commissioner, UK, Cape Town, repeating Bullard's No. 355, DO 119/1275.

9 "A Matter of Political Expediency": The Settlement of Reza Shah's Estate

1 Moodie and Robertson, Solicitors, Pretoria, to Office of the High Commissioner, August 17, 1944, DO 119/1276. A copy of the inventory is attached to J. S. Somers Cocks, British Embassy, Tehran, to Moodie and Robertson, April 25, 1945. See also a clipping from the Rand Daily Mail, September 28, 1944, "Ex-Shah of Persia Leaves £129,317 Estate in Union," which lists the main items in the inventory. Both items are in the same folder.

2 See the list attached to executor's final report, "First Liquidation and Distribution Account in the Estate of the Late Reza Pahlavi," enclosed in McRobert, de Villiers, and Hitge to the High Commissioner, South Africa, January 23, 1947, FO 371/61976.

3 British Embassy, Tehran, to Messrs. Moodie and Robertson, Pretoria, April 25, 1945, DO 119/1276.

4 This sum would have translated into nearly £10 million. The exchange rate in 1941 was 68.8 rials to the pound sterling. The value of the rial fell sharply in the following year and continued to drop during the war.

5 Bullard, Tehran, to Foreign Office, No. 23, April 24, 1945, FO 371/45496.

6 High Commissioner in South Africa, to Dominions Office, No. 604, July 16, 1945, FO 371/45496.

7 The phrase, "return to giver," is Bullard's. See Bullard, Tehran, to Foreign Office, No. 945, September 3, 1945, FO 371/45496; and also Dominions Office to High Commissioner, South Africa, No. 610, September 4, 1945, DO 35/1206.

8 Bullard to Foreign Office, No. 1124, October 12, 1945, FO 371/45496.

9 High Commissioner, South Africa, to Dominions Office, No. 741, September 6, 1945, FO 371/45496; and Moodie and Robertson, Solicitors, Johannesburg, to H. D. Tonking, September 29, 1944, DO 119/1276.

10 High Commissioner, South Africa, to Dominions Office, No. 984, November 21, 1945, FO 371/ 45496; and "Excerpt of Letter from Messrs. MacRobert, de Villiers & Hitge, Solicitors, Pretoria, November 20, 1945 to the Master of the Supreme Court, Pretoria," in DO 35/1206.

11 High Commissioner, South Africa, to Dominions Office, No. 28, January 28, 1947, FO 371/61976.

12 Le Rougetel, Tehran, to Bevin, Foreign Office, No. 474, November 25, 1946, DO 35/1206.

13 Dominions Office to Acting High Commissioner, South Africa, No. 566, November 25, 1946, DO 35/1206.

14 Bullard, Tehran, to Foreign Office, No. 70, July 12, 1945, FO 371/45496.

15 Le Rougetel, Tehran, to C. W. Baxter, Foreign Office, February 26, 1947, FO 371/61976.

16 N. Butler, Foreign Office, to Le Rougetel, Tehran, April 19, 1947, FO 371/61976.

17 High Commissioner, South Africa, to Dominions Office, No. 702, August 27, 1945, E 5118/1077/ 34, FO 371/45496.

18 Bullard, Tehran, to Foreign Office, No. 945, September 3, 1945, FO 371/45496.

19 Secretary, Board of Inland Revenue to the Under-Secretary of State, Foreign Office, January 2, 1947, FO 371/61976.

20 MacRoberts, de Villiers, and Hitge, Solicitors, Pretoria, to the High Commissioner, Cape Town, January 23, 1947, FO 371/61976.

21 Le Rougetel, Tehran, to Bevin, Foreign Office, No. 474, November 25, 1946, DO 35/1206.

22 Le Rougetel, Tehran, to Foreign Office, No. 164, February 1, 1947, FO 371/61976.

23 Le Rougetel, Tehran, to C. W. Baxter, Foreign Office, February 26, 1947, FO 371/61976.

24 MacRobert, de Villiers, and Hitge, Pretoria, to the High Commissioner for the UK in Great Britain, Cape Town, "Re: The Estate of the Ex Shah of Persia," February 23, 1947, p. 3, FO 371/61976.

25 Ibid.

26 Minute on the cover folder of file E1467/10/34, January 23, 1947, FO 371/61976.

27 G. W. Baxter, Foreign Office, to Le Rougetel, Tehran, March 12, 1947, FO 371/61976.

28 Le Rougetel, Tehran, to Foreign Office, No. 550, FO 371/61976.

29 Minute on Le Rougetel's letter by L. F. L. Pyman, Foreign Office, May 6, 1947, E3693/210/34, FO 371/61976.

30 C. W. Baxter, Foreign Office, to the Secretary, Board of Inland Revenue, February 17, 1947, E1058/ 19/34, FO 371/61976.

31 J. F. Huntington, Secretary, Inland Revenue to the Under-Secretary of State, Foreign Office, V.B. 1578/1946, March 10, 1947, FO 371/61976.

32 N. Butler, Foreign Office, to Sir John Stephenson, Dominions Office, E 3693/10/34, May 12, 1947, FO 371/61976.

33 Foreign Office to Tehran, No. 547, July 15, 1947; and Office of High Commissioner, Pretoria, to G. E. Boyd Shannon, Commonwealth Relations Office, London, No. F/27, July 12, 1947, both in FO 371/61976.

34 Foreign Office to Tehran, No. 175, March 22, 1948, FO 371/68726. The process was complicated. In September 1947, the executor of the estate paid the commissioner of internal revenue a sum of nearly £42,000 out of estate funds to cover the estate duty, in anticipation that the money would be refunded once the Parliament voted to approve an additional appropriation. (See J. D. Pohl, Department of External Affairs, South Africa, to H. H. Sedgwick, Office of High Commissioner, Pretoria, September 17, 1947.) The Union government then submitted to the Parliament and secured approval for a remission of death duties of £45,252 (Foreign Office to Tehran, No. 72, February 6, 1948, FO 371/68726). This figure is somewhat higher than the original estimate by the executor of the sum of £43,800 for estate and succession taxes and also in excess of the sum paid by the executor to inland revenue. But this discrepancy may be due to a later recalculation of the value of the estate, expenses incurred, and the taxes due.

35 Commonwealth Relations Office to Foreign Office, No. F 2540/7, December 30, 1947, FO 371/61976; and B. A. B. Burrows, Foreign Office, to Le Rougetel, Tehran, January 24, 1948, FO 371/68726.

36 See minute by L. F. L. Pyman, Foreign Office, January 10, 1948, E12006/1006/34, FO 371/68726.

37 Le Rougetel, Tehran, to Foreign Office, No. 1151, November 8, 1947, and the appended FO minute to this cable, FO 371/61978.

38 The correspondence and materials relevant to the affidavit are in FO 371/68726. The signed affidavit itself is not in the file, probably because it was sent to the Commonwealth Relations Office (CRO) for transmission to the Union government, but a draft that it closely followed is in this file at E 2945/1006/34. The file also contains Le Rougetel's signed and sealed declaration certifying Malik Ismaili's qualifications to issue the affidavit; the cover letter from the British embassy in Tehran to the Foreign Office (E 4854/1006/34), and a letter from the Foreign Office to the Commonwealth Relations Office (also in E 4854/1006/34), dated April 21, 1948, transmitting the affidavit to the CRO.

39 British embassy, Tehran, to Foreign Office, No. G 197/21/48, June 16, 1948.

40 An itemized list of the items shipped is enclosed in H. W. Woodruff, UK Trade Commissioner, Pretoria, August 5, 1948, FO 371/68729.

41 Same to same, No. L 1399, August 5, 1948, FO 371/68729.

Bibliography

Books and Article in English

Abrahamian, Ervand. *Iran between Two Revolutions*. Princeton, NJ: Princeton University Press, 1982.

Afkhami, G. R. *The Life and Times of the Shah*. Berkeley: University of California Press, 2009.

Akhavi, Shahrough. *Religion and Politics in Contemporary Iran: Clergy-State Relations in the Pahlavi Period*. Albany: State University of New York Press, 1980.

Amery, Leo. *The Empire at Bay: The Leo Amery Diaries, 1929–1945*, ed. Leo Barnes and David Nicolson. London: Hutchinson, 1988.

Ansari, Ali M. *Modern Iran: The Pahlavis and After* (Harlow: Pearson, 2003).

Banani, Amin. *The Modernization of Iran, 1921–1941* (Stanford, CA: Stanford University Press, 1961),

Bullard, Reader, *Letters from Tehran: A British Ambassador in World War II Persia*, ed. E. C. Hodgkin. London: Faber and Faber, 1961.

Bullard, Reader. *The Camels Must Go*. London: Faber and Faber, 1961.

Chehabi, Houchang. "Staging the Emperor's New Clothes: Dress Codes and Nation-Building under Reza Shah," *Iranian Studies*, 26, nos. 3–4 (1993), 227, 226.

Clifford, Bede. *Proconsul: Being Incidents in the Life and Career of Sir Bede Clifford*. London: Evans, 1964.

Elwell-Sutton, L. P. "Reza Shah the Great: Founder of the Pahlavi Dynasty," in *Iran under the Pahlavis*, ed. George Lenczowski. Stanford, CA: Hoover Institution Press, 1978.

Ghani, Cyrus. *Iran and the Rise of Reza Shah*. London: I.B. Tauris, 1998.

Gurney, John. "Ann Katharine Swynford Lambton: 1912–2008," in *Biographical Memoirs of Fellows of the British Academy, XII*. London: The British Academy, 2013.

Ironside, Lord, ed. *The Diaries of Major General Sir Edmund Ironside, 1920–1922*. London: Leo Cooper, 1972.

Kadjar (Qajar), Prince Hamid. *Memoirs*, ed. Habib Ladjevardi. Cambridge: Iranian Oral History Project, Center for Middle Eastern Studies, Harvard University, 1996.

Lambton, A. K. S. *Landlord and Peasant in Persia*. Oxford: Oxford University Press, 1953.

Lambton, A. K. S. *The Persian Land Reform, 1962–1966.* Oxford: Clarendon Press, 1969.

Majd, Mohammad Gholi. *Great Britain and Reza Shah: The Plunder of Iran.* Miami: University Press of Florida, 2001.

Pahlavi, Ashraf. *Faces in a Mirror.* Englewood, NJ: Prentice Hall, 1960.

Ramazani, R. K. *Iran's Foreign Policy, 1941–1973.* Charlottesville: University of Virginia Press, 1975.

Skrine, Clarmont. "Assignment to Mauritius," *Blackwood's Magazine*, 275 (January–June 1954).

Wright, Denis. *The Persians among the English.* London: I.B. Tauris, 1985.

Books, Sources in Farsi

Afshar, Amir Aslan. *Khaterat-e Amir Aslan Afshar.* Tehran: Farhang Press, [1991], 2012.

Djam, Fereydoun. *Memoirs* (transcript of interview). Iranian Oral History Project. Cambridge: Center for Middle Eastern Studies, Harvard University, November 24, 1981.

Foroughi, Mahmud. *Memoirs of Mahmud Foroughi*, ed. Habib Ladjevardi. Cambridge: Center for Middle Eastern Studies, Harvard University, 2003.

Mo'tazed, Khosrow. *Az Alāsht ta Ifriqa* [*From Alāsht to Africa*]. Tehran: Enteshārāt-e Dowr-e Donyā Press, [1278] 1999.

Niazmand, Reza. *Reza Shah: Az Tavallod ta Saltanat* [*Reza Shah: From Birth to Kingship*]. Bethesda, MD: Bonyad-e Motela'at-e Iran Press, 1996.

Niazmand, Reza. *Reza Shah: Az Soqut ta Marg* [*Reza Shah: From Fall to Death*]. Tehran: Hekayat-e Qalam-e Novin Press, [1386] 2007.

Pahlavi, Prince Mahmud Reza. Foundation for Iranian Studies, Oral History Project, interview, conducted by Mahnaz Afkhami, Los Angeles, April 18, 1985, https://fis-iran.org/en/content/pahlavi-prince-mahmud-reza.

Safa'i, Ebrahim, ed. *Reza Shah Kabir dar A'ineh-ye Khaterat* [*Reza Shah the Great in the Mirror of Memoirs*]. Tehran: Ministry of Arts and Culture, [2535]/1976.

Saleh, Gholam Hosain Mirza, ed. *Khaterat-e Solayman Behbudi, Shams Pahlavi va Ali Izadi* [*The Memoirs of Solayman Behbudi, Shams Pahlavi and Ali Izadi*]. Tehran: Tarikh-e Now Press, [1372] 1993.

Index